Object-Oriented Programming for AS/400 Programmers

An Introduction with Examples in C++

By Jennifer Hamilton

DUKE PRESS
A Division of
DUKE COMMUNICATIONS
INTERNATIONAL

Loveland, Colorado

Library of Congress Cataloging-in-Publication Data

Hamilton, Jennifer. 1965-
Object-oriented programming for AS/400 programmers : an introduction with examples in C++ / by Jennifer Hamilton
p. cm.
Includes bibliographical references and index.
ISBN 1-882419-05-7
1. Object-oriented programming (Computer science) 2. C++ (Computer program language) 3. IBM AS/400 (Computer) — Programming.
I. Title.
QA76.64.H355 1994
005. 2' 45—dc20 93-48185
CIP

DUKE COMMUNICATIONS INTERNATIONAL
Loveland, Colorado

This book was printed and bound in the United States of America.

ISBN 1-882419-05-7

3 4 5 EB 9 8 7 6

To James,
for surviving the first book and encouraging a second.

Acknowledgements

Many people have contributed to this book, both directly and indirectly. I would like to thank the many attendees of my OOP presentations over the past several years, whose questions and comments have helped me better develop my understanding of the topic and how best to relate it to AS/400 programmers. Thanks to Josee Lajoie and Neville Parakh for their careful review of the C++ section. Paul Conte, through very detailed review of the material, raised many important issues. I would also like to thank and acknowledge the following people for spending time reviewing the material and providing valuable comments and suggestions: Steven Brignoly; Jim Bromley; Andrew Chasin; Ken Chen; Robert Cozzi, Jr.; Jim Crawford; Ann Gawman; Tim Fors; Scott Gerard; James Hamilton; Christopher Jahn; Michael Otey; and Dave Wallace. And thanks to Dave Bernard and Sharon Hamm for working so efficiently to get this project completed on very short notice.

Table of Contents

LIST OF FIGURES VII

PREFACE IX

CHAPTER 1: Introduction 1
Some History 1
Toward OOP 2

CHAPTER 2: Encapsulation 5

CHAPTER 3: Abstraction 9
Abstract Data Types 10

CHAPTER 4: The Object Model 13
General Object Model 13
OS/400 Objects 16
OOP Objects 17

CHAPTER 5: Using Objects 19
Using OOP Objects 20
Adding New Object Types 21
Programming with Objects 22
OK, But...? 26

CHAPTER 6: Classes 29
Classes and Instances 30

CHAPTER 7: Inheritance 33
Methods and Inheritance 35
A Common Code Base 36

CHAPTER 8: Polymorphism 39
Overloading 39
Static and Dynamic Binding 40
Polymorphism 42

CHAPTER 9: A Final Comparison 45

CHAPTER 10: Object-Oriented Programming Languages 49
Simula 49
Smalltalk 50
C++ 50

CHAPTER 11: Classes in C++ 53

CHAPTER 12: Using C++ Classes **57**
Constructors and Destructors **57**
Operator Overloading **60**

CHAPTER 13: Derived Classes in C++ **65**
Protected Class Members **67**
Multiple Inheritance **67**

CHAPTER 14: Additional C++ Constructs **71**
The `friend` Specifier **71**
Virtual Functions **72**
Additional OOP Support **74**
Learning C++ **75**

Afterword **77**

APPENDIX A: The Object-Oriented Architecture of the AS/400 System **81**
System/38 — A High-Level Machine **82**
System/38 Object-Oriented Architecture **90**
System/38 Addressing and Authorization **97**

References **105**

Glossary **109**

Index **111**

List of Figures

Figure 2.1 A Black Box Symbolizing the Concept of Encapsulation 5

Figure 2.2 Software System Defined Using Encapsulation 6

Figure 2.3 Program Design through Functional Decomposition 7

Figure 2.4 Partial Definition and Associated Operations — Modula-2 Module 8

Figure 3.1 Partial Example Using Ada Package `File` to Implement `FileType` 11

Figure 4.1 General Object Model 13

Figure 4.2 OS/400 Object 16

Figure 4.3 OOP Object 17

Figure 4.4 OOP Object DTAARA 18

Figure 5.1 Using OS/400 Objects 19

Figure 5.2 Using OOP Objects 20

Figure 5.3 Adding New OOP Objects 23

Figure 5.4a Date Subroutines and Variables 24

Figure 5.4b Incorrect Variable Access 24

Figure 5.4c Encapsulating Date Subroutines and Variables 25

Figure 5.4d An Object for Each Date Variable 25

Figure 6.1 A Class 29

Figure 6.2 Classes and Objects 31

Figure 7.1 Inheritance 33

Figure 7.2 Redefining Superclass Method 36

Figure 7.3 Superclass Change Propagated to Subclasses 37

Figure 8.1 Binding to Class Code 41

Figure 8.2 Polymorphism 43

Figure 9.1 The OS/400 and OOP Object Models 45

Figure 9.2 OS/400 Architecture and Implementation 47

Figure 11.1 A C++ Class Definition 54

Figure 11.2 Using the `dtaara` Class 55

Figure 12.1a Defining a Constructor and a Destructor for Class `dtaara` 58

Figure 12.1b Class `dtaara` Member Function Definitions 59
Figure 12.1c Using a Class with a Constructor and a Destructor Defined 59
Figure 12.2a Partial Definition for the Class `date` 61
Figure 12.2b Overloading Operators 62
Figure 12.3 Using Operator Overloading 63
Figure 13.1 Syntax for Defining a Derived Class 65
Figure 13.2 A Simple Derived Class 66
Figure 13.3 Using the Access-Specifier `protected` 68
Figure 13.4 Syntax for Defining a Derived Class with Multiple Inheritance 68
Figure 13.5 Multiple Inheritance 69
Figure 14.1 Using the `friend` Specifier 72
Figure 14.2a Defining a Virtual Function 73
Figure 14.2b Program Output 74

Preface

This book is not intended to be an exhaustive discussion of the field of object-oriented programming (OOP) — there are many other books that do that. Nor is the purpose to teach how to do object-oriented programming using the AS/400 system. Rather, the objective is to introduce AS/400 programmers to basic object-oriented programming concepts through simple, easy-to-understand explanations using the OS/400 object model as a basis for the discussion.

Object-Oriented Programming for AS/400 Programmers introduces and explains fundamental object-oriented programming concepts, such as objects, classes, inheritance, and polymorphism. When you finish reading this book, you should have an understanding of what these concepts mean with respect to both object-oriented programming and the OS/400 operating system, and why these concepts are important for improving how we design and develop software.

The book has two main sections. The first section (Chapters 1 through 9) introduces you to OOP. This discussion of OOP concepts is language independent, so you will find it useful regardless of the particular programming language you may be interested in using. The second section (Chapters 10 through 14) introduces you to the C++ object-oriented programming language. This section provides concrete illustrations of the concepts by introducing the C++ language through a series of examples modeled on the OS/400 object model. An appendix comprises reprints of several articles that describe the design goals and object-oriented architecture of the OS/400 operating system.

— *JAH*

CHAPTER 1

Introduction

The term *object-oriented* has become a buzzword in the 1990s. Rarely can you flip through a computer-related magazine without coming across it, either in articles discussing the concepts and applications, or in advertisements exhorting it as an advantage a particular product enjoys. The term is used freely to symbolize anything good; as Roger King has pointed out, if you want to sell something, you should simply stress that it is object-oriented: "I have a cat named Trash. In the current political climate, it would seem that if I were trying to sell him (at least to a computer scientist), I would not stress that he is gentle to humans and is self-sufficient, living mostly on field mice. Rather, I would argue that he is object-oriented" [King89].

In this book, I will discuss one part of the field of *object-oriented computing*: object-oriented programming (OOP). However, much of the discussion will apply to other areas of this field, such as object-oriented databases and user interfaces, the unifying concept being that of the object. The terms and concepts that I introduce throughout the book are summarized in the "Glossary," page 109, which you may find a useful reference as you read through the chapters.

SOME HISTORY

Object-oriented programming is among the most recent attempts to solve what has been called the "software crisis." Since the recognition of this crisis in the late 1960s, many techniques and methodologies have been introduced to deal with and attempt to solve it.

The three main facets of the software crisis are that

- the need for software far exceeds the ability to produce it;
- it is rare for a software project to be finished on time and under budget; and
- the cost of maintaining or extending existing software is very high.

Part of the problem is that software is inherently complex; and as we witness rapidly increasing hardware capabilities and user demands for software to take advantage of these capabilities, the complexity increases. So instead of improving the situation, increased hardware capability is actually making it worse.

Although many of the attempts to deal with the software crisis (such as structured programming methodologies and data flow analysis) have certainly improved our ability to develop software, in general we find ourselves still working from scratch. With many applications, it is often cheaper to completely rewrite a software product than to make major extensions to, or attempt to reuse pieces from, an existing one.

As one answer to the software crisis, the goal of object-oriented programming is to design and write systems that can easily be reused and extended, to reduce the cost of producing and maintaining software. Reusing existing software would, first, decrease development time and cost, which in turn would help reduce the complexity of the project as a whole; second, maintenance costs would decrease because the proven software would have fewer bugs than new software. This combination would address the software backlog issue, because more development resources would then be available.

Despite the media hype, however, I don't claim that OOP will solve the world's software problems. Developing software will continue to be a difficult job, but as you will learn, OOP shows much potential in making that job easier.

Toward OOP

Because of the publicity, you are probably feeling pressure to understand and take advantage of this seemingly new technology that promises to save the world so that programmers can have a weekend off now and then. I am assuming you are familiar with the OS/400 object model, so I will use it as a basis for the discussion, comparing the OS/400 and the OOP object models throughout. This serves two purposes: first, to leverage your existing knowledge and provide a familiar context for the examples (OOP objects and OS/400 objects have much in common, so you're ahead of the game if you're an AS/400 or S/38 programmer); second, to explain where the models are different. Most (if not all) OOP books and courses don't discuss the OS/400 object model, so AS/400 programmers who have been exposed to such media are often left asking questions such as "How do OS/400 objects relate?" and "Does the OS/400 object support imply that the operating system is written using an object-oriented programming language?"

Although the widespread appearance of object-oriented programming in the media has been relatively recent, the concepts are not new. Object-oriented concepts build on and are strongly based in existing software engineering concepts, most notably *encapsulation* and *abstraction.* Hence, the OOP approach is considered evolutionary rather than revolutionary. In fact, the first programming language to include many of today's OOP concepts was Simula, which was designed in the early

1960s. However, it wasn't until the more recent availability of OOP languages, such as Smalltalk and C++, on PC and UNIX platforms, that language support for this programming methodology became available to the average programmer.

I will begin our discussion of object-oriented programming with an explanation of encapsulation and abstraction in Chapters 2 and 3, respectively. To illustrate these concepts, I show how two earlier programming languages, Modula-2 and Ada, support them, while subsequent OOP-specific discussions will refer to examples in C++.

CHAPTER 2

Encapsulation

As we discussed in Chapter 1, one of the two primary software engineering concepts upon which object-oriented concepts are built is that of *encapsulation*. In 1972, David Parnas introduced the concept of encapsulation, also called *information hiding*. Parnas proposed that software be designed by breaking it down into modules, where a module is essentially a black box (Figure 2.1) that is well defined in terms of its inputs, result, and side effects (if any). These characteristics together form the interface for the module.

A module is defined with regard to a design decision that is hidden from all other modules in the program. A module typically hides something that is likely to change, such as the format of a data structure or the details of performing some task. (Note that a module is independent of the physical program structure, representing a single programmer's task rather than a subprogram.)

A module's specification should

- provide the user all the information needed to use the program correctly, and nothing more;
- provide the implementer all the information about the intended use necessary to complete the program, and no additional information;
- be formal enough so that it can conceivably be machine-tested for consistency, completeness, and other desirable properties; and
- discuss the program in terms familiar to both the user and the implementer.

FIGURE 2.1
A Black Box Symbolizing the Concept of Encapsulation

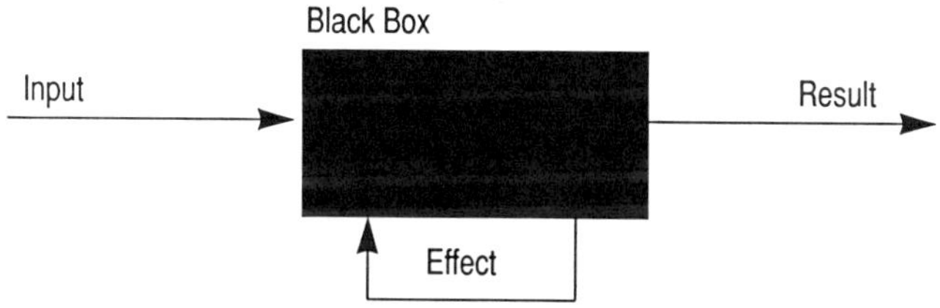

In other words, the module specification should hide, or *encapsulate*, the module implementation details.

A *module interface guide* documents the system design and the interface to each module and becomes the bible for the software development project. No knowledge of a module's implementation details is visible in the documented interface. To use a module created by someone else, a programmer needs to understand only the module's documented interface. This approach reduces the amount of detail the programmer must comprehend and, more importantly, avoids dependencies upon the implementation of that module.

The goal of this design methodology is to produce a software system defined completely in terms of modules, as the diagram in Figure 2.2 shows, thus reducing overall software cost by allowing modules to be designed and revised independently. A given module can be modified or completely replaced; so long as the new module conforms to the interface, the change will not affect the rest of the system.

This method of software design differs from the more widely used approach of functional decomposition, in which a problem is successively broken down into smaller subproblems until the subproblem is a manageable size for a programmer, as shown in Figure 2.3. The data manipulated by the software system is typically shared across the various subprograms that make up the system. Functional decomposition is widely used because it is fairly well understood and relatively easy to apply to many different problem domains. Its major drawback is that sharing data across the system results in high interdependencies, or *coupling*, between the subprograms, making it difficult to reuse select portions of the software, or to modify the underlying data representation without requiring widespread code changes.

FIGURE 2.2
Software System Defined Using Encapsulation

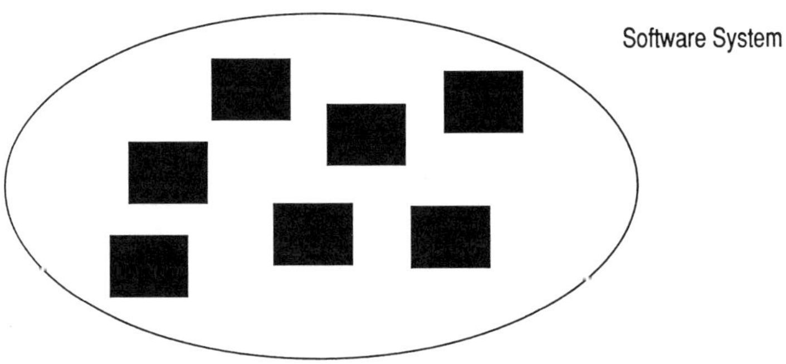

FIGURE 2.3
Program Design through Functional Decomposition

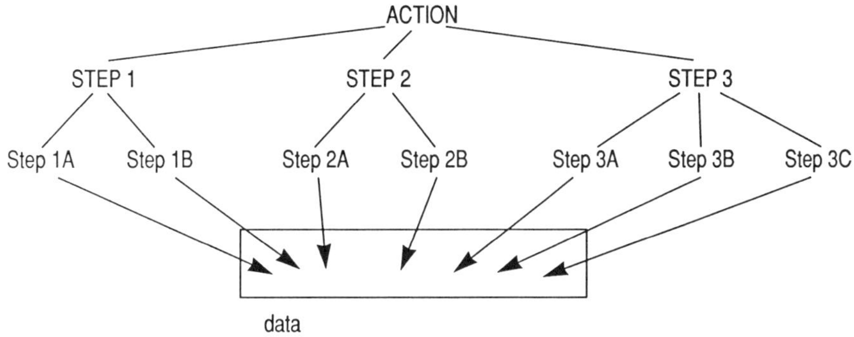

It can be very difficult to define modules in such a way that they are simple and sufficiently functional, but also such that changes to the system do not require changes to the interfaces, thus causing system-wide changes. An intrinsic part of OOP involves designing systems in this way; thus the field of *object-oriented design* has evolved to address this and other challenges related to designing object-oriented programs.

Some languages provide support for encapsulation. For example, Modula-2 supports encapsulation through its *module* language construct. A Modula-2 module is defined by two parts: a *definition* part and an *implementation* part. The definition part specifies the portion of the module that is accessible outside the module, and the implementation part specifies the hidden part of the module. Other parts of the program can refer only to information contained in the definition part; the Modula-2 compiler prevents references from outside the module to anything in the implementation part. This construct allows related data and procedures to be grouped together formally and allows data to be shared across related procedures in a controlled way.

Figure 2.4 shows a partial definition of a Modula-2 module, `File`, and its associated operations. The definition module defines several boolean variables (e.g., `IsEof`, `IsOpen`) that can be used to test the state of the file, along with the operations `Open`, `Chain`, and `Write`. The implementation module specifies the details for implementing the `File` module. Another module, in this example the main program in the module `main`, can import information from the definition part. The implementation part, however, is hidden, and nothing in it can be referenced or accessed outside the `File` module. Thus, the `File` details in the implementation module are encapsulated by the definition module.

FIGURE 2.4
Partial Definition and Associated Operations — Modula-2 Module

```
DEFINITION MODULE File;
     VAR IsEof, IsRecNotFound, IsOpen: BOOLEAN;
     PROCEDURE Open( ... );
     PROCEDURE Chain( ... ): record;
     PROCEDURE Write( ... );
END File;
```

```
IMPLEMENTATION MODULE File;
     VAR file: FILE;

     PROCEDURE Open( ... );
     BEGIN
          IF (* file opened successfully *)
               IsOpen := TRUE;
     END Open;

     PROCEDURE Chain( ... );
     BEGIN
          IsRecNotFound := FALSE;
          IF (* can't find record *)
               IsRecNotFound := TRUE;
     END Chain;

BEGIN
     IsEof := FALSE;
     IsOpen := FALSE;
     IsRecNotFound := FALSE;
END File;
```

```
MODULE main;
     FROM File IMPORT
          IsEof, IsRecordNotFound, IsOpen, Open, Chain, Write;
BEGIN
     Open("FILE1");
     recread := Chain("KEY1");
     IF IsRecordNotFound THEN
          (* show value *)
END main;
```

CHAPTER 3

Abstraction

To complete our initial discussion of the primary software engineering concepts on which object-oriented programming is based, let's look now at the concept of *abstraction*. An abstraction is "a simplified description, or specification, of a system that emphasizes some of the system's details or properties while suppressing others. A good abstraction is one that emphasizes details that are significant to the reader or user and suppresses details that are, at least for the moment, immaterial or diversionary" [Shaw84].

Abstraction is a powerful technique we use every day to deal with the world. For example, when you drive a car and turn the steering wheel counterclockwise, your conceptualization of this action is that it will turn the car to the left. To perform this operation, you need not consider, or even be aware of, the fact that the steering wheel is connected to the steering shaft, which is connected to the steering gear, which is connected to the steering linkage, which is connected to spindles about which the wheels rotate. You do not need to appreciate the series of mechanical operations that take place between these components and transform turning the steering wheel into turning the car.

If you had to learn and be aware of all these details for every action, driving a car would be much more complicated than it already is. This abstraction also lets us drive cars that have very different underlying mechanisms, such as rack and pinion steering versus worm and sector steering, because our understanding of how to drive is not based on the underlying mechanical details, but rather on a high-level abstraction of the car. The "interface" remains the same: You turn the wheel counterclockwise to go left and clockwise to go right.

The concept of abstraction can also help us deal with software. Rather than needing to understand all the underlying details of a piece of software, we can use abstraction to consider only the necessary information. You are likely familiar with, and have used, one form of programming abstraction: *procedural abstraction*. Such an abstraction lets us consider a sequence of arbitrarily complex operations as a single operation. An RPG subprogram that calculates and returns a value is an example of a procedural abstraction. Most modern programming languages support a mechanism for procedural abstraction.

Abstract Data Types

A *data abstraction* or *abstract data type* combines the concepts of encapsulation and procedural abstraction to define a set of data items and associated operations in an abstract way. The only defined way to operate on the type is through the specified operations, which are defined in such a way as not to reveal or require an understanding of the underlying representation of the data.

An abstract data type provides the programmer with a new data item and a way to manipulate it, without requiring or allowing the programmer to understand or depend upon the implementation or representation of that data item. For example, most programming languages support built-in arithmetic types, such as integers, and operations on those types, such as addition and multiplication. When programmers use these operations, they do not need to understand or even be aware of how an integer is represented or of the algorithms used to perform the arithmetic. Also, the operations defined on the type are sufficient to manipulate the data without requiring knowledge of these details.

As an example of an abstract data type, consider the RPG/400 file type. Only certain operations, such as OPEN and WRITE, are valid for a file. You cannot issue an operation such as ADD against a file, because ADD is not in the set of valid operations. Also, there is no defined mechanism that lets the programmer access the underlying structure used by the language runtime to represent that type (i.e., the file information block (FIB) and the user file control block (UFCB)).

Using an operation defined for an RPG/400 file neither requires nor in any way depends upon this underlying representation. When you perform a CHAIN operation against a file, you need know only that the CHAIN will perform a random-access read operation against the file, returning the desired record, if found, or an error indication otherwise. You do not need to understand the underlying structures used to represent the file, nor what steps the language runtime and the operating system must take to actually perform that operation.

Some languages provide facilities that let you create abstract data types as *user-defined data types* that the compiler treats as a built-in type in terms of variable declaration and usage. Languages that support user-defined data types provide a powerful mechanism for formally representing the internal structure of a program. Programming languages such as Ada, through its *package* construct, support user-defined data types as the means for programmers to implement new abstract data types.

Figure 3.1 shows a partial example of using an Ada package, `File`, to implement an abstract data type, called here `FileType`. The package specification defines the interface to `FileType` and defines several

FIGURE 3.1
Partial Example Using Ada Package `File` to Implement `FileType`

```
package File is
    type FileType is limited private;
    procedure Open(file: in FileType; ... );
    function Chain(file: in FileType; ... ) return Record;
    procedure Write(file: in FileType; ... );
    function IsRecNotFound(file: in FileType) return BOOLEAN;
    function IsOpen(file: in FileType) return BOOLEAN;
    function IsEof(file: in FileType) return BOOLEAN;

private
    type FileType is
        record
            eof: BOOLEAN;
            isopen: BOOLEAN;
            recnotfound: BOOLEAN;
            .
            .
            .
        end record;
end FileType;
```

```
package body File is
    -- implementation details
    procedure Open(file: in out FileType; ... ) is
    begin
        if -- file opened successfully -- then
            file.isopen = TRUE;
    end;
end File;
```

```
with File;
procedure MAIN_PROGRAM is
    use File;
    file1, file2: FileType;
begin
    Open(file1, "FILE1");
    Open(file2, "FILE2");
    recread = Chain(file1, "KEY1");
    if IsRecNotFound(file1) then
        -- show value
end MAIN_PROGRAM;
```

operations. Specifying `limited private` with the type declaration indicates that no operations are allowed on that type except by calling the routines listed in the package specification. The package body defines the implementation details of the `File` package. The procedures and functions declared in the body can directly manipulate the private type `FileType`. The main program declares two variables of type `FileType` and uses them with the operations defined for that type.

A user-defined data type differs from the module concept in Modula-2 in that, for example, an Ada package can introduce a type that the compiler can manage, so you can create multiple instances of the data item through a declaration. To allow new instances of a file to be declared and managed, Modula-2 would need to support a procedure such as `Create` or `New`. In Modula-2, you cannot simply declare a variable of type `File` as you can in Ada. And the programmer, rather than the compiler, is responsible for managing the storage associated with Modula-2 types. With language support for user-defined data types, you can declare new variables of the given type using standard declaration syntax, and the compiler will manage the variable as it does the built-in types, along with enforcing the defined encapsulation.

You may be familiar with languages such as Pascal and C, which allow their built-in types to be extended in a limited way by letting you specify a description of a data item as a type. You can then declare variables of that type such that the compiler will treat them, in terms of scope and storage management, as built-in types. However, such type definition support differs from support for user-defined data types in two important ways. First, there is no support for encapsulation: The compiler cannot prevent unintended access to the underlying representation of the type. Second, there is no explicit association between the operations used to manipulate the type and the type itself, so the intended association is not readily obvious.

You do not need to use a language that directly supports the techniques of encapsulation and data abstraction to use the techniques themselves. For example, I can write a set of RPG subroutines that operate on a data structure, where the data structure and subroutines together represent an abstract data type.

There is, however, an important distinction between those languages that support and those that enable a technique. Bjarne Stroustrup differentiates the two this way: "A language *supports* a programming style if it provides facilities that make it convenient (reasonably easy, safe, and efficient) to use that style. A language does not support a technique if it takes exceptional effort or skill to write such programs; in that case, the language merely *enables* programmers to use the technique" [Stro88]. So a language such as Ada that supports user-defined types typically makes it easier for the programmer to write a program using abstract data types than does a language such as Pascal, which requires more management by the programmer.

Chapter 4

The Object Model

In the previous two chapters, I discussed the software engineering concepts of encapsulation and abstraction, which form the basis for the object model. In this chapter, I explain what an object is and how the object-oriented programming and OS/400 object models relate.

The concept of the object model has evolved over the past two decades through fairly independent work in several areas of computer science, including programming languages, databases, and user interfaces. Although the object-oriented approach has proved very useful in dealing with the inherent complexities of various types of systems, the diverse origins of the object model have resulted in much discrepancy with respect to terminology and exactly what object-oriented means. Even within the field of object-oriented programming, many languages define the same concepts using different terminology. The definitions I use throughout this book are based on those proposed by Wegner [Wegn87] and Nelson [Nels91] which are generally accepted in the object-oriented programming field.

General Object Model

I'll first describe what I call the general object model, which is a system-independent description, and then discuss the OS/400 and OOP object models with respect to this general model. In Chapter 2, I introduced the concept of encapsulation and described a means of program design where the system is defined in terms of black boxes or modules, the details of which are encapsulated by the module interface. An object is essentially such a black box, consisting of two parts: a hidden part and a visible part (Figure 4.1).

Figure 4.1
General Object Model

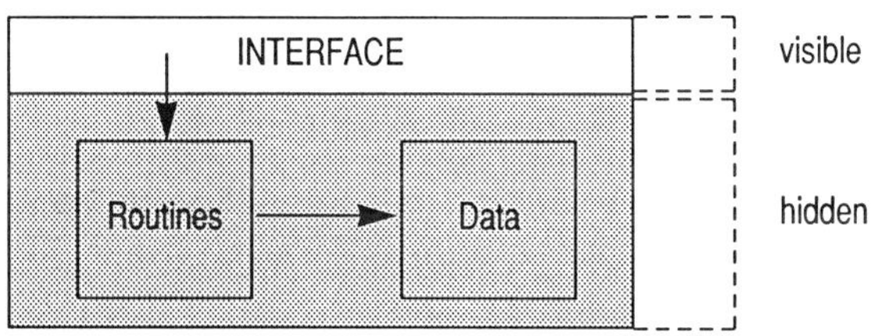

The hidden part, which is typically the majority of the object, consists of data and routines that operate on that data. The hidden portion of an object is not accessible outside of that object, so only the internal routines that make up the hidden part of the object can operate directly on the underlying data. This encapsulation allows changes to be made to the internal representation of the object, isolating code changes to only those internal routines that are allowed to directly access the hidden portion.

The visible part is the interface to the object; the only defined way to access the data and routines that are hidden in the object is through the interface. The interface is a set of callable operations that are used to manipulate the object. (Note that some systems allow variables to form part of the interface, which is not considered good programming practice; but I restrict the discussion to callable operations only.) Recall from Chapter 3 that abstraction is a means of describing a system in a simplified way, reducing the complexity of understanding the system by considering only the relevant details and hiding the rest. The operations that make up an object's interface are defined using abstraction, so as to not reveal any of the details that are hidden in the object, and to limit the information required to manipulate the object to only the relevant details.

Thus, the object model encompasses encapsulation and abstraction to completely define hidden data and abstract operations on that data. The basic concept here is to associate the data and the routines that operate on that data with each other, so that the only way to directly manipulate the data is through the interface.

The object model is a powerful concept; by designing software in terms of objects, we can

- change underlying data representations without causing widespread code changes throughout the system,

- simplify the system by breaking it down into manageable pieces, which allows us to consider only the relevant portions rather than having to understand the whole system to deal with one aspect,

- greatly reduce the interdependencies between the pieces that make up the software system, thus providing a greater opportunity for code reuse than if the pieces were dependent on other parts of the application for their functionality,

- improve software robustness by taking advantage of the decreased interdependencies to more thoroughly test the pieces independently, and

- simplify problem-determination; because if an object's data is corrupted, there are a limited number of places (i.e., the object's internal routines) where that could have occurred.

Typically, a variable declared to be of one of the built-in types in a programming language is a kind of object; the physical representation is hidden and there is a restrictive set of abstract operations you can apply to that variable. A file in an RPG program is a good example of such a variable. The underlying data structures and routines used by the compiler to represent and manipulate the file are hidden; and the only defined way to access them is through the valid operations on that file object, such as CHAIN and WRITE. These operations are defined in abstract terms that don't depend upon the underlying hidden implementation of the file. The RPG programmer has no access to or dependency upon these underlying structures and routines.

This design gives the supplier of the file object, the RPG compiler developers, great freedom to modify the underlying representation of a file, because no code other than internal compiler code can be dependent upon that representation. Also, because the operations are defined in abstract terms and not dependent upon the details of the file, such as the file type, (i.e., DISK or PRINTER), the RPG programmer needs only one name for a given operation, such as WRITE, that applies to all file types rather than having to learn specific operation names for each file type.

By contrast, a data structure in an RPG program is not an example of an object, because the subfields that make up the data structure are not encapsulated by the data structure and can be accessed throughout the program using a variety of mechanisms, rather than through a controlled interface consisting of abstract operations.

A system that supports and enforces the concept of objects as described above is called *object-based.* (An *object-oriented* system is one that is object-based and also supports the concepts of *classes* and *inheritance.* I will discuss these concepts in further detail in Chapters 6 and 7, but will use the term object-oriented throughout except where I want to restrict the discussion to only the object-based concepts.)

In terms of programming languages, the Ada and Modula-2 languages are examples of object-based languages. Through the package and module constructs respectively, discussed in Chapter 2, these languages support and enforce the general object model.

Note that an object is not intended to be a security mechanism to prevent intentional access to hidden data. Rather, the goal is to 1) prevent inadvertent access to, and dependency on, the underlying details; and 2) eliminate the need to understand those details before using the object.

OS/400 Objects

Now let's take a look at the OS/400 object model, which most of you should be familiar with. An OS/400 object, as shown in Figure 4.2, consists of three components: the physical object itself, the operating system programs that operate on the physical object, and the set of CL commands that can be used to invoke those operating system programs.

The OS/400 object model fits into the general model described above. The operating system programs and the physical representation form the hidden part of the object, and the CL commands form the visible interface to the object. The only defined way (and with security level 40, the only possible way) to manipulate the object is through the defined CL command interface. (For some object types, the interface also includes HLL operations and APIs; but for simplicity I restrict the discussion to the CL commands.) An OS/400 programmer has no access to nor dependency upon the underlying representation of the object. The CL command interfaces themselves are defined in abstract terms and do not reveal the underlying implementation of the object.

For example, consider an OS/400 data area object. There is no mechanism, such as obtaining a pointer to the actual data in the physical object, through which an OS/400 programmer can directly manipulate the data area object. The only defined way to create and manipulate such an object is indirectly, through the defined CL commands, such as CRTDTAARA and CHGDTAARA. These operations in no way reveal the underlying implementation used to represent and manipulate the physical object. Thus, the details of the representation of the physical data area are encapsulated by the abstract CL command interface.

We can therefore say that the OS/400 operating system is object-based because it enforces and supports the concept of objects. This object-based support is a major strength of the AS/400 system, allowing the operating system developers great flexibility to take advantage of new software and hardware technology. Because no OS/400 program-

Figure 4.2
OS/400 Object

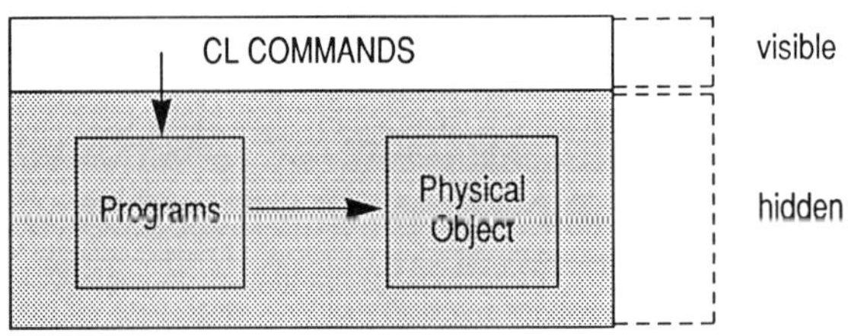

mer can inadvertently be dependent upon, for example, how an index object is represented and manipulated, this change can be made without concern for its impact on existing applications if a more efficient representation is discovered.

Such a design provides an advantage for both the object user and supplier — in this case, the AS/400 customer and IBM, respectively. The user has a fixed interface that protects his/her software investment as new releases of the operating system are made available, but that allows for new implementations to be introduced. And the supplier is able to move to new technology in an upwardly compatible way.

OOP OBJECTS

An object-oriented programming object, as shown in Figure 4.3, consists of a set of operations and associated internal data and routines, packaged together as a single logical entity. All the code and data required to represent and manipulate the object are explicitly associated together. The operations defined for an OOP object are called *methods*. The set of methods defined for an object together form the visible, abstract interface to the object. (The term *method* does not imply an implementation; it's simply the terminology used to refer to the name of an operation associated with an object.)

An OOP object also fits into the general object model described earlier. The internal data and routines form the hidden part of the object; the only defined way to access the hidden part of an object is by invoking one of the methods for that object.

As an example, Figure 4.4 shows an OOP object modeled after an OS/400 DTAARA object. The methods for the object are CRTDTAARA, CHGDTAARA, and DSPDTAARA; and these methods are the only way to manipulate the underlying data that represents the data area. No knowledge or understanding of the routines invoked by the methods, or the storage representation of the data, is visible or required. The data

FIGURE 4.3
OOP Object

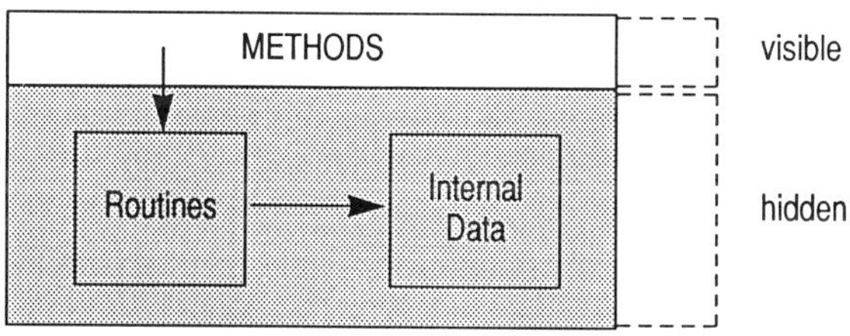

FIGURE 4.4
OOP Object DTAARA

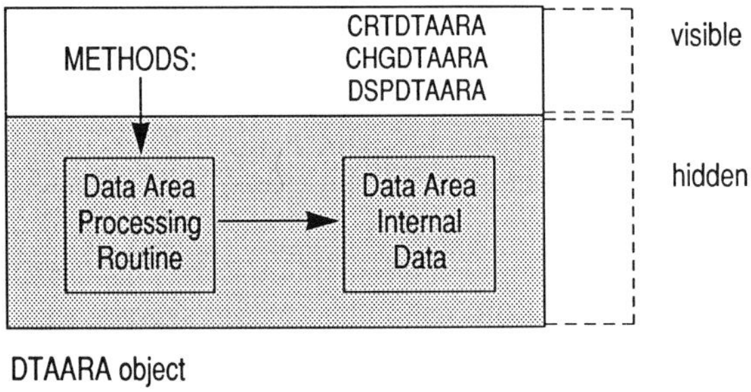

representing the DTAARA object is explicitly associated with and shared between the methods for manipulating that object.

CHAPTER 5

Using Objects

To help you better understand the OOP model, let's discuss the OS/400 object model in more detail. Using an OS/400 object follows the *operator/ operand* model: A program (operator) acts upon the object (operand). The operator determines the appropriate processing to perform based on the object type. The operand is considered passive and must be acted upon by the active operator.

Consider a CL command such as CHGDTAARA that changes the value of a given data area. As shown in Figure 5.1, the CL command is called and given the name of the data area to change along with the new value for that data area. A single, specific processing program is directly associated with the command called to handle the request. This program is always called to change the value of any type of data area.

To process the command, the processing program must first look for the named object and ensure that there is a data area by that name. If successful, it must then determine the appropriate processing based on the data area type. Note that this latter operation requires that the program know all possible data area types. If a new data area type was to be added, such as a date data area, all such programs (e.g., for create, display, etc.) must be modified to handle this new type. Instead of the code changes being localized in one place — in the object — they would be spread out across the system (that is, in the type selection code of each of the processing programs.)

FIGURE 5.1
Using OS/400 Objects

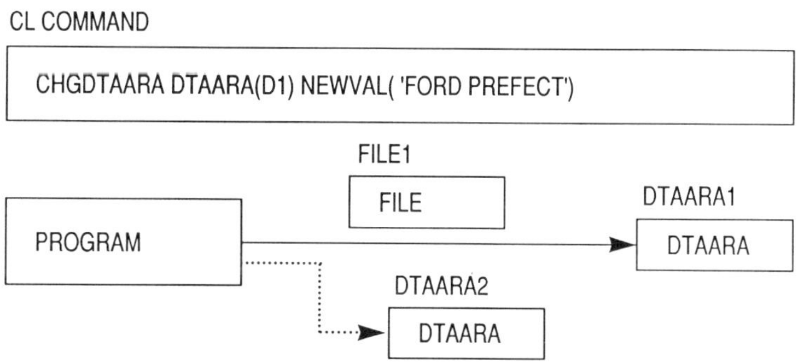

Using OOP Objects

To operate on an object, you invoke one of its methods. This is called *sending a message* to that object. (This process does not imply concurrency, nor is there any direct equivalent in the OS/400 object model.) Sending a message to an object is a form of indirect call. Rather than naming a routine to be called directly, you send the object a message and in turn it calls the appropriate method. The message consists of the operation to be performed (the method name) and any parameters to be passed.

For example, consider a program that reads an OS/400 data queue and responds to various requests. The requests are in the form of a 15-character string, such as 'UPDCUSTINFO'. When a program adds an entry to the queue to request an operation, the server will examine the name of the operation and call the appropriate routine to perform the request. The actual routine called may have a totally different name from the operation requested. That is, the 'UPDCUSTINFO' request could result in the UCUST subroutine being called by the server. Thus, the requesting program has indirectly called a routine in the server program instead of directly calling a named routine. Also, two different server programs could respond to the same operation request by calling totally different underlying routines.

Figure 5.2 shows how a CHGDTAARA operation would be issued with an OOP object. A message is sent to the object, requesting that the object invoke the CHGDTAARA method to change its value to the new

FIGURE 5.2
Using OOP Objects

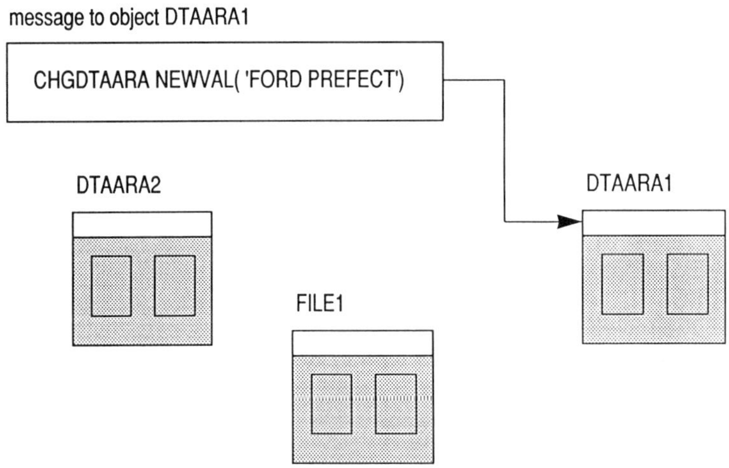

value provided. The object will perform whatever processing is appropriate to its type. The object itself does not need to be aware of the existence of any other objects or object types — it only deals with its own internal data. Using an OOP object follows the *message/object* model: A message is sent to an object to request that it invoke one of its methods. The entire OOP object is considered to be an active entity: Instead of a passive operand being manipulated by an operator, you tell the active object to manipulate itself by sending it a message.

The operator/operand model differs from the message/object model in two important ways:

1. With the operator/operand model, type dependencies are spread across the system, in each of the operators. The operator selects the operation to perform, based on the type of the operand. With the message/object model, type dependencies are isolated to the object.

2. Invoking an operator causes the specific named routine to be called. In general, calling the same routine with different parameters always results in that same routine being called. Sending a message is a form of indirect call. The message specifies the operation to perform, and the object selects the method to invoke based on the message. In this way, different objects can respond in different ways to the same message.

Adding New Object Types

The advantages of object-oriented programming become apparent as we attempt to extend or modify existing code. An OOP object is considered to be a single logical entity, consisting not only of the internal data, but also of the methods and internal routines for manipulating the object. An OOP object's internal routines only deal with that object's data. The components making up an OS/400 object, by contrast, are not packaged together. The CL commands are separate from the processing programs they call, which are separate from the physical object residing on the system. A given processing program can operate on many different objects. This distinction makes the message/object model more flexible than the operator/operand model when adding new object types.

Using the OS/400 operand/operator model as a base, consider the processing routine for a command such as DSPFD. Because this processing routine is called for all file types, it would have logic such as the following:

```
if object is dspf then
    call dsp_dspf(object)
else if object is savf then
    call dsp_savf(object)
else if object is faxf then
    call dsp_faxf(object)
.
.
.
```

This processing routine is dependent upon each file object type in the system. If a new type of file was to be added, such as `faxf`, this routine, and all others containing similar logic, would need to be changed to reflect the new type. The changes would be spread across the system, in each separate type-dependent processing routine — not localized to one place.

With an OOP object, as shown in Figure 5.3, all the processing code is in one place: with the object itself. Instead of calling a specific procedure that determines what to do with the object based on the type, as shown above, the OOP object decides what to do based on the message sent, as in

```
if message is dsp then
    call dsp_this_object
else if message is chg then
    call chg_this_object
.
.
.
```

When we add a new object type, we define the data and all the methods for operating on the object together, grouped as a single logical entity. The existing code continues to send the display message to the object regardless of its type, and the object itself is responsible for displaying only its own data. The new object does not need to be aware of any other types of objects in the system, and no other code in the system needs to be changed or made aware of the new object type.

Programming with Objects

At this point, you may be wondering how to identify an object to send it a message. Typically, the programmer has some form of handle that represents the object. The message is sent to the object by operating on that handle. In object-oriented programming languages (OOPLs) an

FIGURE 5.3
Adding New OOP Objects

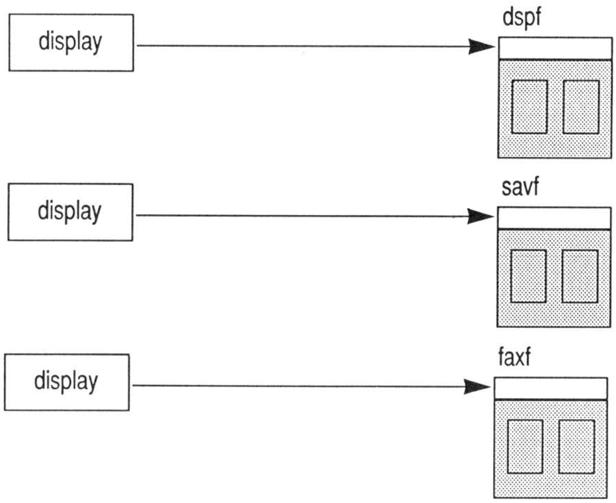

object is a variable; a message is sent to an object using the variable name. In Chapter 11 I will discuss how to create and use objects in the C++ language.

From a programming perspective, an object in an OOPL is much like a variable in standard programming languages, except that it has user-defined routines associated with it through which you operate on the data, rather than just the language-supplied routines. Given the definition of a user-defined type from Chapter 3, a variable declared to be of such a type is an object. Instead of the data in the object being directly manipulated using the language-supplied operations, as is done with a normal variable, the associated user-defined operations must be called to perform the manipulation.

As discussed in Chapter 3, you do not need language support for object-oriented programming to write object-oriented applications. Object-oriented programming is defined by how you design your software rather than by the language you use to write the software. In particular, you can certainly write object-based applications in languages such as RPG and COBOL. A good example of this is the OS/400 operating system — it is object-based, but it is written in a standard 3GL language. The more language support you have for concepts such as encapsulation, however, the easier it is to write such a program.

For example, suppose you are going to write a set of date-handling routines. You can design your program structure as shown in Figure 5.4a. The code for the program consists of those date routines and the code for the rest of the program, and the variables in the program consist of the variables that represent dates and some other variables used by the rest of the program. The intention would be that only the date routines themselves will manipulate the date variable internals, and that the date routines will manipulate only these date variables. That is, you don't want a situation like that shown in Figure 5.4b, where date routines are accidentally operating on the wrong variables or the rest of the program is manipulating the date variables directly, thus possibly corrupting their values or creating a dependency upon their representation.

With the OOP model, you essentially draw a black box around the

FIGURE 5.4A
Date Subroutines and Variables

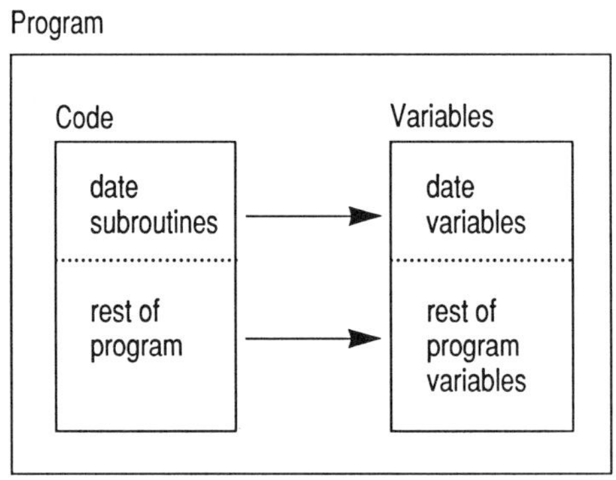

FIGURE 5.4B
Incorrect Variable Access

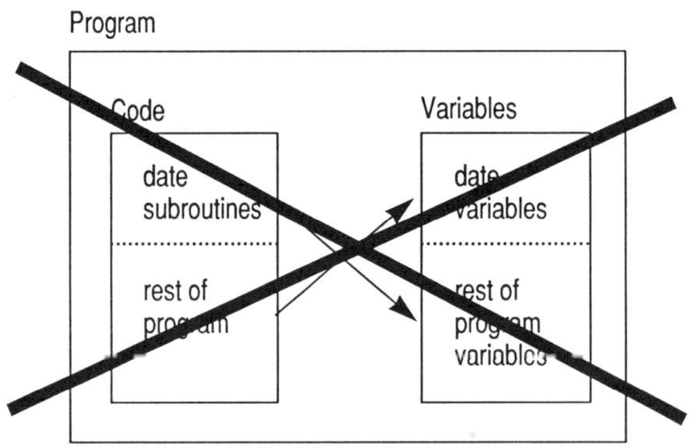

date variables and routines as shown in Figure 5.4c, preventing access to the box except through the defined interface (the subroutines). The operations in the interface are defined using abstraction. The result is that each date variable is treated as an object, as shown in Figure 5.4d. Then, if you wanted to change, for example, the format used to represent a date, you could do so knowing that only the date operations would be affected, and not the rest of the application (as long as you maintained conformance to the interface). You gain the same advantages as the RPG compiler and OS/400 operating system developers mentioned earlier: the freedom to update underlying structures and routines

FIGURE 5.4C
Encapsulating Date Subroutines and Variables

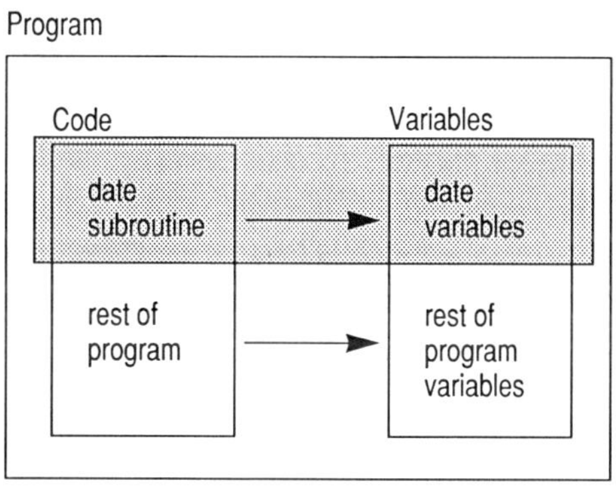

FIGURE 5.4D
An Object for Each Date Variable

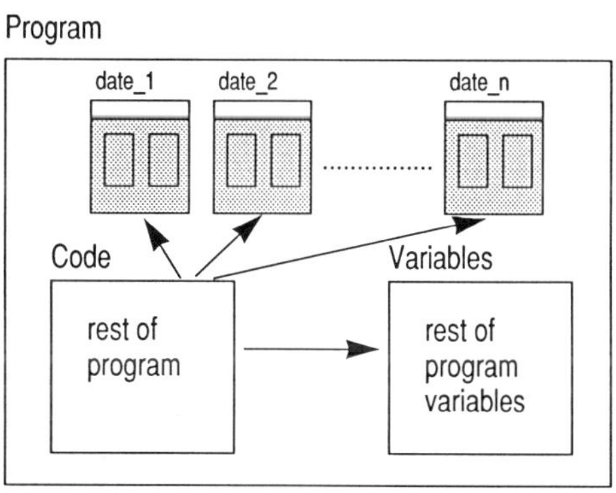

with limited impact. Another advantage of this design is that those date routines become reusable components that you can simply plug into another application that needs date support, because the use and representation of the date variables is isolated and not dependent upon any other code in the program.

You can certainly implement this design in a language such as RPG, but you will have to enforce the encapsulation yourself. That is, there is no construct in the language to allow you to define data and associate subroutines with that data in such a way that the compiler will prevent access to the data except through those subroutines. And if you have several different types of dates you want to process with the same operation, you must write code that determines what to do based on the object type. An OOPL such as Smalltalk or C++ will manage all this for you.

OK, But ...?

At this point, you may have one or more of the following concerns:

- If the object consists of the data and associated code, and if I have three data area objects, does that mean I have duplicate copies of all that code for each object?
- If the code for two object types (such as DSPFD for a DSPF and a SAVF) is basically the same, with some differences, do you have to duplicate the common code for each object type?
- What are the performance implications of object-oriented programming?
- I still don't see how the message/object model is any different from just calling a routine and passing the object as a parameter.
- How does structured programming relate to object-oriented programming?

The answer to the first concern is that the code is not duplicated for each object in the system, although *logically* you can consider it to be. All objects of a given type belong to the same *class.* A class is an abstract data type; it defines the data structure and routines that make up both the visible and hidden parts of an object. All objects of the same class share the code for that class, so physically the code is not duplicated, but logically you can treat objects as if they have their own copy of their class code. I will cover the class concept and how this code sharing takes place in Chapter 6.

With respect to the second concern, object-oriented programming languages support the concept of *inheritance,* which is the expression of the difference between a new object and an old object such that all the common processing code can remain in one place. I will cover inheritance in Chapter 7.

In terms of performance, an overhead is associated with object-oriented programming. In the previous example of the RPG date subroutines and variables, there is a cost associated with making a subroutine call to access a variable compared to accessing the variable directly. In general, a substantially larger number of calls are taking place in object-oriented programs than in procedure-oriented programs. This overhead is one of the reasons object-oriented programming has not seen widespread use until recently, because generally available computers have not been fast enough to support such programs. Object-oriented programming is another trade-off between programmer productivity and program performance that has been an issue since software development began. For example, when FORTRAN was developed in the 1950s, there was much skepticism about the viability of high-level languages with respect to compile-time and run-time efficiency compared to that of assemblers. Today, writing code in an assembly language is certainly the exception rather than the norm, because programmers can be so much more productive with high-level languages, even though a program written completely in an assembly language may run faster.

The fourth concern often comes from looking at the implementation rather than the concept. Ultimately, sending a message to an object does invoke a routine, but this is an indirect call and does not cause an explicit named routine to be invoked. The same message sent to different objects can result in totally different routines being called. Remember that an object has methods associated with it; instead of a routine being called and passed an object, selecting what to do based on the object type, the object selects one of these methods based on the message.

Language support versus enablement also adds to the confusion: To implement this message/object model in a language that does not support objects, you only have standard procedure calls with which to work. To be able to send the message display to several different object types, you must at some point have logic that determines the object type and calls the appropriate processing routine. This is how the OS/400 operating system implementation was described earlier. An object-oriented programming language, however, can manage the types implicitly, so you can have several different display methods, each associated with a different object type; and the compiler will handle the message routing, implicitly determining the appropriate method to call by examining the object itself.

In response to the final concern, although OOP is a "new" way to write programs, with OOP we are not abandoning the lessons of structured programming. OOP encompasses structured programming, the many rules and guidelines of which still apply and are used when writing the internal object routines.

CHAPTER 6

Classes

A *class* is a template that describes one or more similar objects. The class describes both the visible interface to and the hidden portion of an object. All objects have a single corresponding class that defines the valid methods for and the underlying structure of that object. An object belonging to a certain class is called an *instance* of that class. All objects of the same class have the same interface and underlying structure, but each object has unique storage associated with it. The class description, then, is essentially like a cookie-cutter, used to construct physical objects that look the same.

For example, Figure 6.1 shows the class DTAARA, which defines the common interface and underlying structure of the three physical DTAARA objects shown below the dashed line. These three physical objects are all instances of the class DTAARA. The class defines the valid methods for the objects, such as CRTDTAARA and CHGDTAARA, along with the underlying structure of all DTAARA objects, (perhaps a variable length piece of storage that could represent either character, numeric, or binary data), and the code for manipulating that data. All three DTAARA objects have the same set of methods as defined in the class description, and are identical in every respect except for the data stored in them.

The class concept is consistent with the OS/400 object model: All objects of the same type, such as SAVF, have the same set of CL

FIGURE 6.1
A Class

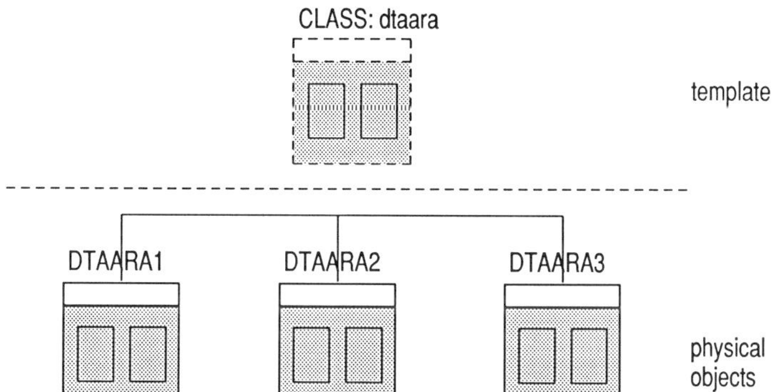

commands that are valid for them, which are those defined for SAVF objects. They also have the same underlying structure, but the actual data they contain can be different. Although the term 'type' is used rather than 'class' to describe similar objects in OS/400 terminology, the concepts are basically the same.

In object-oriented programming languages, a class defines an abstract data type as a user-defined type that is treated by the compiler like a built-in type in the language. You use the user-defined type support to define the underlying structure of the objects and to associate operations with the data. When you declare a variable using a user-defined type, such as the variables declared of type `FileType` in Figure 3.1 (Chapter 3), that variable is an object, and the compiler will enforce the encapsulation of the object's data so that the only way to access it is through the interface defined in the class.

In Chapter 11, we will see how to define and use a class in the C++ language. If you'd like, you can jump ahead to that chapter (page 53) for a concrete example of the C++ class construct, and then return to this point to continue the discussion.

Classes and Instances

So far, we have been treating an object as a single logical entity consisting of both data and the code to manipulate it. In Chapter 5, I mentioned a concern that having three DTAARA objects would mean there would be three copies of the DTAARA code in the system. Each object doesn't really have a copy of the code, but you view it logically as if that were the case. What is actually happening is that the code for an object is associated with the object's class, and all objects of the same class share that code.

Figure 6.2 illustrates how this works. In the center of the picture is a class, which contains a description of the data for objects of that class, along with the code used to manipulate an object's data. The class does not have any physical storage associated with it. Each object belonging to that class, on the other hand, contains a unique copy of the physical storage for the object's data, corresponding to the structure defined in the class, but does not actually contain a copy of the code. Instead, each object shares the code defined in the class. When a message is sent to an object, the associated class code for that object is invoked, and that class code will operate on the data for the current object. An object-oriented programming language will handle the invoking of the appropriate class code for a given object. From the outside, however, as shown in the far upper right of the picture, the object is viewed as if it did contain both the data and the code. When a message is sent to the object, it appears that the object contains the code to manipulate itself.

FIGURE 6.2
Classes and Objects

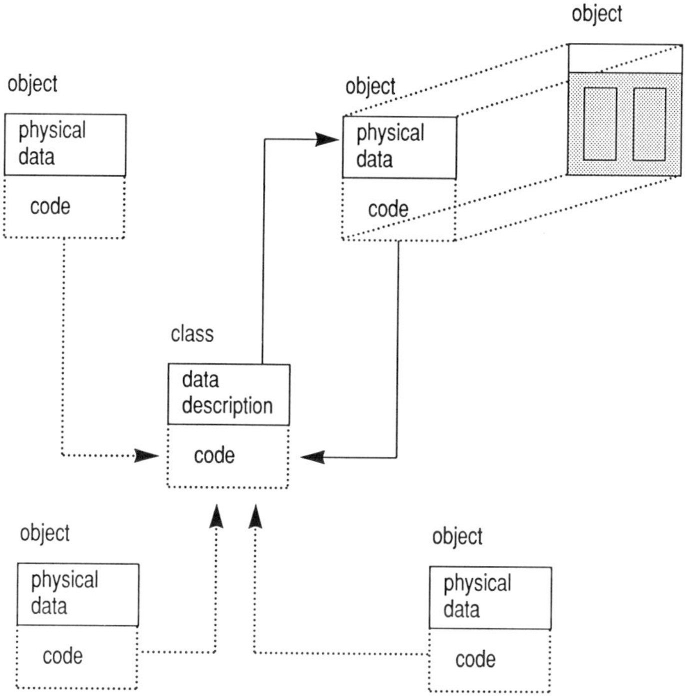

However, it is the class code that operates on the data for that particular object that is actually invoked.

The class construct is an important mechanism for reuse in object-oriented programming. Because the class represents a self-contained definition of the hidden and visible parts of an object, the class represents a pluggable entity that you can insert where needed. For example, suppose you have an application that needs to manipulate dates. You can define a date class, which contains the operations valid for date objects, such as add_date and sub_date, the underlying structure of the storage used to hold the date value, and the code to manipulate that data. All the code for describing and manipulating a date object is contained in that class description, and the rest of your application code has no access to nor dependency on the underlying structure defined in the date class. The next time you write an application that requires date manipulation, you can simply plug the date class from your first application into the new application. You can use the same code base for both applications; so if you find a bug in the class code, you can fix it in one place rather than having to maintain multiple copies of the code. And voilá, code reuse!

Another benefit of classes is that you can define multiple classes with the same interface, but with different underlying implementations, perhaps with different runtime or space implications. You can switch between different classes in the program, depending upon your requirements, without requiring massive code changes, because the interfaces are the same. An example of this in the OS/400 operating system is physical and logical files. The interfaces to these two types of objects are basically the same, but they have different underlying characteristics. You can change a program that operates on a physical file to operate on a logical file instead, without requiring widespread changes to your program, because the interfaces are the same.

A class library is a collection of one or more classes. Most object-oriented programming languages supply class libraries to perform operations such as screen I/O or maintaining collections of objects. There is also a growing industry in vendor-developed reusable class libraries. So instead of having to write your own date class, you may be able to purchase a class library from a vendor. You could either use it "as is," or extend it using inheritance — the topic of the next chapter — and write only a small amount of new code.

CHAPTER 7

Inheritance

The class construct provides a strong mechanism for code reuse in object-oriented programming. *Inheritance* is another powerful mechanism for reusing code through extension. Inheritance is basically a code-sharing mechanism that allows a new class to be defined with respect to an existing class, without physically copying the code. Inheritance allows you to express the difference between an existing class and a new one, keeping all the common portions in one place — in the existing class — and adding the new information only in the new class.

When a new class inherits from an existing class, all objects of the new class will contain any data defined in both the new and the existing class, and any methods valid against objects of the existing class are valid against objects of the new class. The existing and new classes are called the *superclass* and *subclass*, respectively.

To illustrate this concept, Figure 7.1 shows a class hierarchy roughly modeled on the OS/400 object model. At the top of the hierarchy is what I will call the BASE class, which represents the common attributes

FIGURE 7.1
Inheritance

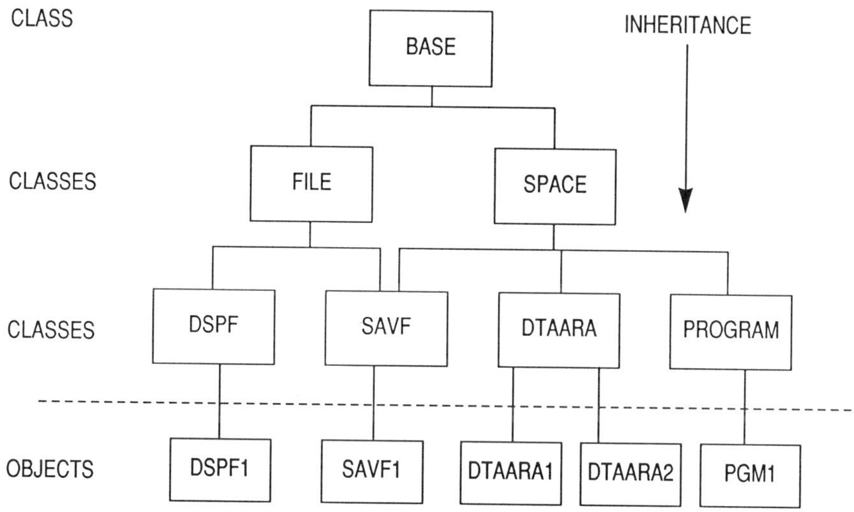

and methods of all OS/400 objects. For example, all objects have a name, an owner, and a type. And certain methods are valid against all objects, regardless of type, such as DSPOBJD and RNMOBJ. All such attributes and methods are defined in the BASE class.

Directly below the BASE class, on the left, is the class FILE, which inherits from the class BASE. This means that a FILE object will have all the attributes of a BASE object (e.g., a name and an owner). Any method defined in the BASE class is inherited by the FILE class, so you can apply DSPOBJD or RNMOBJ against a FILE object. The FILE class need only define the attributes and methods that are specific to FILE objects, such as the file type attribute and the method DSPFD. No code in the BASE class needs to be modified to take into account the fact that a FILE class has inherited from it, nor is any code in the BASE class duplicated in the FILE class. The relationship between FILE and BASE is called an "is-a" relationship; a FILE object is a BASE object, with some modification.

Inheritance does not break the encapsulation defined for a class. When a subclass inherits from a superclass, anything that is hidden in the superclass cannot be directly accessed through code in the subclass. For example, if the object name and type are hidden data items in the BASE class, accessible only through BASE class methods, the code in the FILE class must use those methods to access that information and cannot directly access the hidden data.

To the right of the FILE class is the class SPACE, which also inherits from the BASE class. So a SPACE object is also a BASE object, consisting of any data defined in the BASE and SPACE classes. And any method valid against a BASE object is valid against a SPACE object. Again, no code from BASE is duplicated in the SPACE class — all code for handling BASE object attributes and behavior resides only in the BASE class.

Below the FILE class are the classes DSPF and SAVF, both of which inherit from the class FILE. Inheritance is transitive, so any data and methods inherited from the BASE class by the FILE class are inherited by the DSPF and SAVF classes, along with any additional data and methods defined in the FILE class. A DSPF object is a FILE object and is a BASE object.

Note that the SAVF class inherits from both the FILE and the SPACE classes. This is called *multiple inheritance*; a SAVF object will include data and methods defined in both the FILE and SPACE classes, along with those of the BASE class. Multiple inheritance in itself is a fairly simple concept, in that a subclass simply has more than one direct superclass, but it can be tricky to support; in particular, the situation where the same method name is defined in more than one superclass. This name collision is handled in a variety of ways, depending upon the language or system.

At the very bottom of the figure are physical objects, which are instances of the various subclasses. From the outside, the physical objects are no different from the objects we discussed in the previous chapters. Each object has exactly one corresponding class. All instances of a given class are structurally the same, consisting of the data defined for that class, with the same set of valid methods; and they share the code for that class. The only difference is that some of the data and code may be defined in a superclass rather than directly in the actual class of which the object is an instance.

In Chapter 4, I defined an object-based system as one that supports and enforces the concept of objects. An *object-oriented* system is an object-based system that also supports the concepts of classes and inheritance. In terms of programming languages, Smalltalk and C++ are examples of object-oriented languages, because they both support all three concepts of objects, classes, and inheritance. Both Modula-2 and Ada are object-based, as we discussed in Chapter 4, but neither is object-oriented, because they do not support inheritance.

Chapter 13 discusses the C++ support for inheritance, through *derived classes.* You may find it useful to read the first section of that chapter on page 65 now, for a concrete example of using inheritance in an object-oriented programming language, and then return to this point.

Methods and Inheritance

When one class inherits from another, a method defined in the superclass can be redefined in the subclass. For example, as shown in Figure 7.2, the class FILE inherits the methods from the BASE class, such as DSPOBJD, CRTDUPOBJ and RNMOBJ, along with any data defined in the BASE class. Two new methods are supplied in the FILE class: DLTF and DSPFD. DLTF deletes a FILE object, and DSPFD displays the common header information associated with a FILE object, information that is maintained by the FILE class. The two classes DSPF and SAVF inherit from FILE, which means they include any data and methods defined in the FILE class or inherited from the BASE class.

In the OS/400 object model, DLTF performs the same action regardless of the actual file type; but DSPFD displays different categories of information depending upon the file type. So to follow that model, we would want to inherit the DLTF method as is, but would want DSPFD to act differently for DSPF and SAVF objects, according to their type. You can do this by supplying a new version of the DSPFD method in the subclass. So the DSPF class can simply supply its own version of DSPFD for display file-specific behavior, as can the SAVF class, overriding that version in the FILE class.

FIGURE 7.2
Redefining Superclass Method

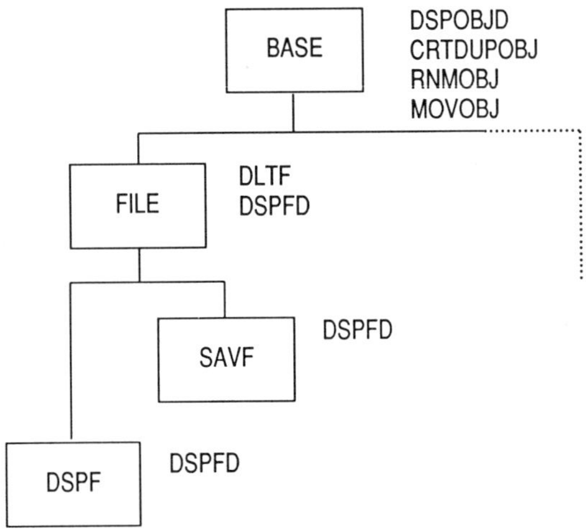

Common processing would still be done by the version of DSPFD in the FILE class, however, and you would not want to duplicate this code in the subclasses. To avoid this duplication, a subclass method can invoke a superclass method on itself, so that the common processing can still be handled in one place. For example, the version of DSPFD in the DSPF class, when invoked, could call the DSPFD method in the FILE class to display the common header information, and upon return would display the information specific to display files.

All subclass objects always include any data defined as part of the superclass; but you can exclude methods, so that not all methods of the superclass are inherited by the subclass. For example, following the OS/400 object model, you cannot issue a CRTDUPOBJ against a DTAQ object; so if you create the DTAQ class by inheriting from the BASE class, you would exclude that method so it could not be applied against DTAQ objects. But the DTAQ subclass would always include any data defined in the BASE class, so a DTAQ object would always have a name and an owner, etc.

A Common Code Base

Note that there may be situations where you want to define a class for which there will never be any instances created; the class is defined only to create a common base for other subclasses to inherit from. Such a class is known as an *abstract* class. For example, following the OS/400 model, there is no such thing as just a BASE object (it must be, for example, a DSPF or DTAARA object), but by defining the BASE class and inheriting from it, we can use it to maintain and represent the common attributes of all objects.

Inheritance allows information to be maintained in one place, reducing the need to duplicate information. Through inheritance, code can be extended more easily, maintaining a common base without the need to duplicate code. Inheritance also allows global changes to be made to many classes by updating only a common superclass, rather than updating each class individually. A good example of this is the concept of object domain and program state that was added to all OS/400 objects a few releases back. Each object was assigned a domain of either system or user, and a system domain object can only be accessed from a program running in system state. Using the inheritance model, the concept of object domain can be added to the BASE class, as shown in Figure 7.3, and it will be automatically propagated down to all other classes in the system. No code in the subclasses needs to be modified to be aware of this new attribute; all code for handling is added in one place, in the BASE class.

Now, depending upon the system or language, you may need to recompile the code that manipulates the subclasses, so that such new information will be available. With the OS/400 system, because objects are persistent, the only time such a global change could be made is on a release boundary. When objects are restored to the new release, the domain attribute would be added to them. However, this again illustrates the power of the OS/400 encapsulated object support: Such changes can and have been made without having an impact on existing programs.

FIGURE 7.3
Superclass Change Propagated to Subclasses

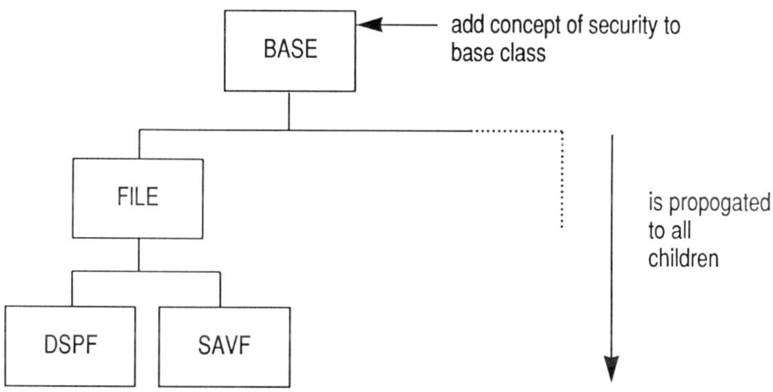

CHAPTER 8

Polymorphism

This chapter discusses the final object-oriented programming concept we will be covering: *polymorphism.* But first, I will cover two related topics: overloading and binding.

OVERLOADING

Overloading is a simple concept you are probably already familiar with. Overloading means you can use the same operator or name for multiple operand types, and the appropriate code is invoked depending upon the operands specified. For example, the + operator can be used in the C language to add both integer and floating-point numbers; there is not a special operator for each different operand type. However, the underlying arithmetic performed due to overloading is very different. The overloading refers to the fact that the operator is being used to represent more than one underlying function — in this case, both integer and floating-point addition.

Some languages, such as Smalltalk and C++, allow you to overload existing operators to be used with new object types. For example, if you define a class for manipulating dates in C++, you could overload the + operator to be used with date objects and supply the appropriate code to be called to handle the date addition. The appropriate routine would be called to handle the addition depending upon the type of the operands. For example, you could use it as follows:

date2 = date1 + increment;

It is fairly clear that the purpose of the above statement is to increment one date variable, date1, and assign the result to another date variable, date2 more readily understood than if the operator couldn't be overloaded and you had to call a function, such as the following:

date2 = add_date(date1, increment);

Another advantage of operator overloading is that there are fewer new things for the programmer to learn. If you want to increment a date variable, you don't have to look up a function name, you simply use the well-known + operator. For an example of defining and using an overloaded operator in the C++ language, see the section "Operator Overloading" on page 60 of Chapter 12.

The overloading of function and procedure names follows the same concept, but it can be more flexible. An operator is defined to accept a certain number of operands. For example, + requires two operands; so when you overload this symbol, you would typically define it to require two operands, to be consistent with the common understanding of that operator. With *name overloading,* you overload the name to be used with different operand types and you are more free to specify different numbers of operands. The underlying code to invoke is determined by the type and number of arguments passed. When name overloading isn't supported, you must either have a single operator with type-sensitive logic (following the operator/operand model we discussed in Chapter 5); or you must have type-specific names, where the type of the operand is incorporated into the operand name.

The RPG language includes many examples of name overloading. With the CLEAR operation code, you can specify many different operands in factor 2, and the compiler will perform different actions depending upon the operand type. There is not a special operand with the type name incorporated for each type, such as CLRDS and CLRRF — just the single operation code CLEAR. As an RPG programmer, you only have to learn that one new operation code. With CLEAR, you can specify, for example, a record format name or an indicator, and a different action will be taken depending upon the type (clear all fields in the record format based on field type or set the indicator to '0', respectively.)

Another example is the DELET operation code. You can omit factor 1 and just specify a value in factor 2, in which case the current record will be deleted. Or you can specify a relative record number or key in factor 1 in addition to factor 2, which will cause that particular record to be deleted. Again, the programmer need only learn one operation code, DELET, and can specify optional additional parameters depending upon the type of deletion desired.

The concept of a subclass redefining a method in its superclass is also an example of overloading. In Chapter 7, the method DSPFD was overloaded in the FILE, DSPF, and SAVF classes. Overloading has the advantage of simplifying the programmer's interface by requiring the programmer to learn the minimum number of new things; and as we shall see when we discuss polymorphism, overloading allows a great deal of flexibility in dealing with different object types.

Static and Dynamic Binding

In the discussion of classes in Chapter 6, I explained that the code for an object isn't physically duplicated for each object; rather, each instance of a class shares the code for that class, as shown in Figure 8.1. When a

FIGURE 8.1
Binding to Class Code

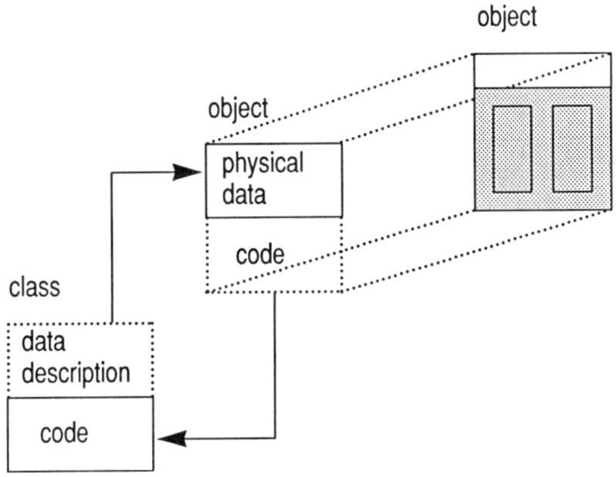

message is sent to an object, the compiler must determine the code to invoke based on the object's class. The key issue is when that decision is made, and it can be made at one of two points: either at program-creation time or at runtime. *Static binding,* or *early binding,* means that the specific method to be invoked when a particular message is sent to an object is determined at program-creation time. The compiler will generate some form of direct link to the code for the target method at the point where the message is sent, and that target code must exist when the calling program is created. This is similar in concept to calling a subroutine in an RPG program. At program-creation time, the RPG compiler generates a branch to the subroutine name when an EXSR operation code is encountered. If that particular subroutine does not exist in the program, an error is flagged at program-creation time.

With *dynamic binding,* or *late binding,* the particular method to be invoked is not determined until runtime, when the message is actually sent to the object. The target method does not have to exist when the calling program is created. This is similar to calling a program using the RPG CALL operation code. It is not until the first CALL operation code to the program is actually executed, at run-time, that the target program is resolved to, and that target program does not have to exist when the calling program is created.

As you are no doubt aware, dynamic binding provides a great deal of flexibility over static binding, but there is certainly some overhead involved. In most object-oriented programming languages, the overhead of dynamic binding isn't nearly that of an RPG CALL (which is due in part to the extra work, such as authority checking, performed by the OS/400 operating system); but dynamic binding, to varying degrees, does incur a performance penalty.

POLYMORPHISM

Polymorphism simply allows the same method name to be overloaded in different classes. Languages that support polymorphism alleviate the need for type-selection code. You can define a given method name in multiple classes, and the appropriate actual method is selected implicitly by the language, based on the target object type. Without language support for polymorphism, the programmer must write type-selection code to be able to use the same name with different object types.

In object-oriented programming languages, polymorphism combines overloading and dynamic binding so that the same message can be sent to different object types; but the binding to the method is not performed until runtime. Using polymorphism, you can treat an object in a generic way, regardless of its type. For example, using the inheritance model discussed in Chapter 7, suppose you had a program that manipulates different kinds of objects, such as managing lists of files associated with particular applications. At some point in the program, you may want to display the description for each file in a particular list; so you would like to have logic something like the following in the program:

for each object in the list
send message "DSPFD" to object

Each object type (DSPF, SAVF, etc.) will have its own version of the DSPFD method that should be invoked, as shown in Figure 8.2, so the generic statement above must determine which method to invoke. Without dynamic binding, there would no way to achieve this, because with static binding, a message can only be bound to one particular method. Using the combination of overloading and dynamic binding that is polymorphism, the same message can be sent to different object types, and at runtime the appropriate method is invoked based on the object type.

The C++ language supports polymorphism through the virtual function construct. For an example of this, see the section "Virtual Functions" on page 72 of Chapter 14.

Polymorphism is the power behind the message/object model, allowing the same message sent from the same point in a program to invoke completely different methods. It can be viewed as a form of abstraction away from the class or type details of a particular object. The program using the object need only be concerned with the operation to be performed, for example DSPFD, and not the underlying type of the object.

Another advantage of polymorphism is the ability to introduce new

FIGURE 8.2
Polymorphism

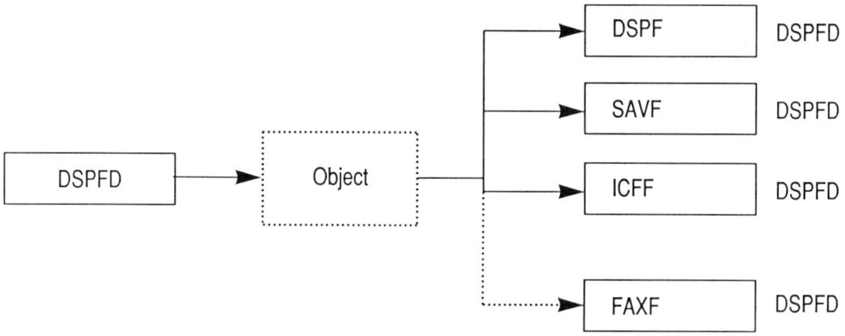

object types into existing programs, without having to recompile the program. For example, given the program described above, if we created a new class called FAXF, as long is this new class included a DSPFD method, a FAXF object could simply be introduced to the existing application and added to the appropriate list. When the DSPFD message is subsequently sent to the FAXF object, as shown in Figure 8.2, polymorphism ensures that the FAXF class method is invoked.

CHAPTER 9

A Final Comparison

This chapter completes the introduction to object-oriented programming concepts. Throughout the discussion, I have been comparing the OS/400 and OOP object models, and have used OS/400 examples to explain OOP concepts. Before I continue with object-oriented programming languages and the introduction to C++, I want to do a final comparison of the two models to make it clear where they are similar and where they differ.

Figure 9.1 depicts the OS/400 and OOP object models. Both models encompass encapsulation and abstraction to support and enforce the

FIGURE 9.1
The OS/400 and OOP Object Models

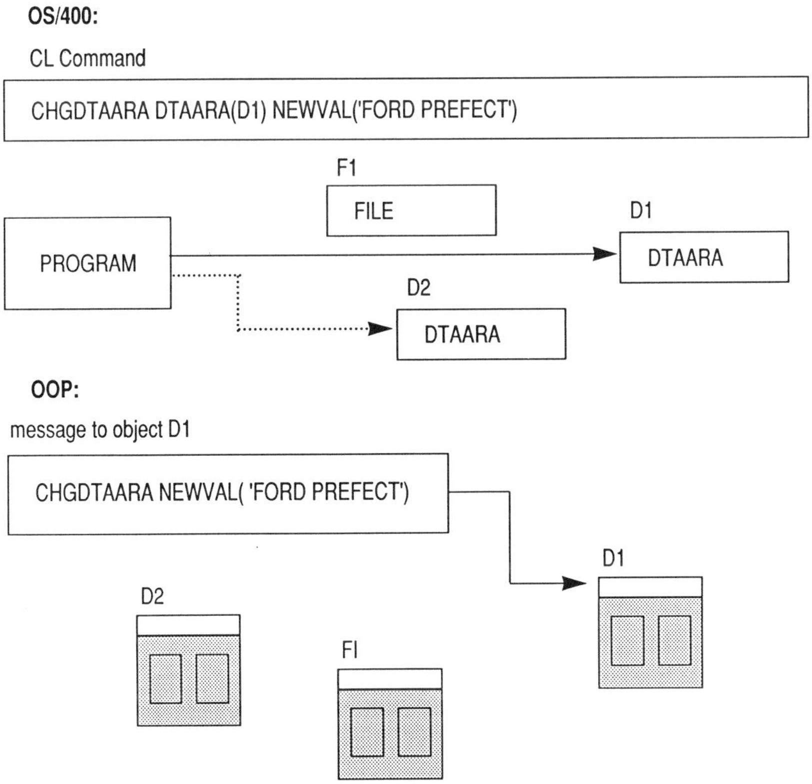

general object model as described in Chapter 4. This is where the two models are the same: in the support of objects. Where they differ, however, is in how the objects are used.

The OS/400 operating system follows the operator/operand model, where a single operator handles multiple operand types and, hence, such operators must include type selection code. When a CL command is invoked against an object, invoking that command results in exactly the same program being called, regardless of the object type, because a given CL command can have only one associated processing program.

With object-oriented programming, on the other hand, through overloading and polymorphism using the message/object model, a message is sent directly to a target object. That object handles that message for itself through the methods defined in the associated class, and is not dependent upon any other object types. Type dependencies are localized to the class code for that object. Unlike the AS/400 model, a particular message sent to an OOP object could result in one of any number of actual methods being invoked, depending upon the target object type.

The OS/400 model is not polymorphic, because there is only one physical routine, containing type-selection code, corresponding to a given CL command. The OOP model is polymorphic, because you can define the same method name in multiple classes and the actual method invoked will be determined implicitly based on the target object type. Polymorphism alleviates the requirement for type-selection code.

Also, an OS/400 object is considered a passive entity that must be operated on by a processing program. An OOP object, however, is considered to be an active entity — you send it a message to tell it to invoke one of its methods, rather than treating it as a passive entity that is passed as a parameter to a type-dependent operator.

Now, let's consider the OS/400 operating system itself. Figure 9.2 represents the OS/400 operating system 's architecture and implementation. In other words, I'm considering the design model for the operating system — the architecture — and comparing it to the implementation of that model — the operating system code that is shipped with the system.

We can say that the OS/400 architecture is object-oriented, because it includes the concepts of objects, classes, and inheritance. Although it's not actually defined as such in the system documentation, there is a concept of a BASE class in the architecture, from which all other object types inherit attributes and methods, along with other superclasses such as those discussed in Chapter 7.

The OS/400 implementation, however, is only object-based. It does support the concepts of objects and classes, but there is no inheritance. OS/400 programmers can create and use objects according to the object

FIGURE 9.2
OS/400 Architecture and Implementation

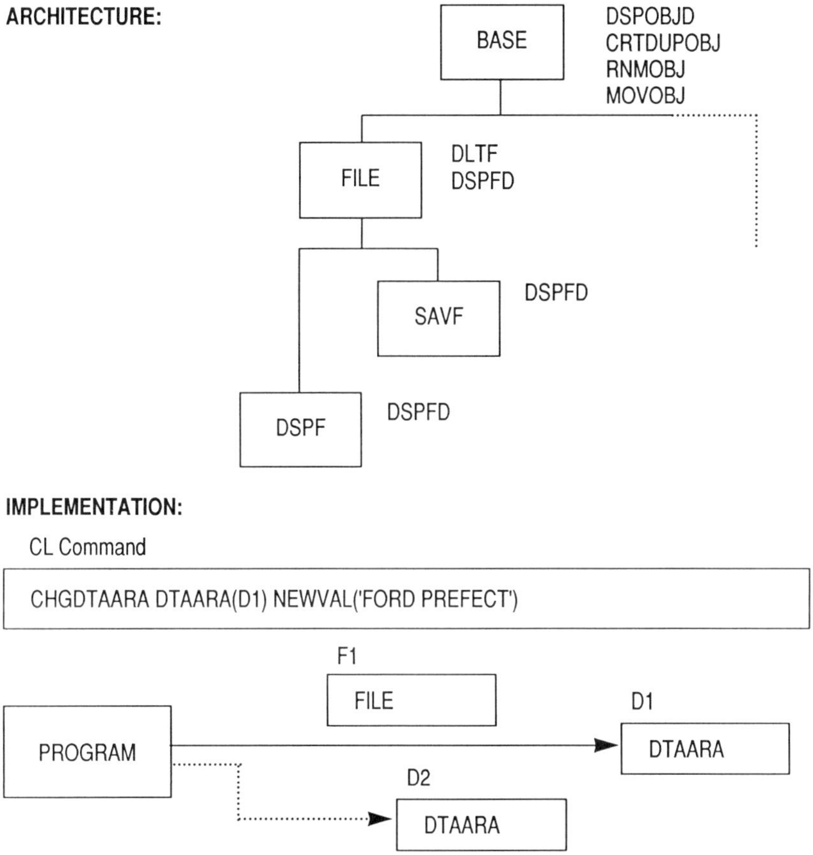

model described in Chapter 4, but they cannot create new object types (classes) and inherit attributes and programs from the IBM-supplied objects. For example, you cannot create a new data area class, such as a date data area, and inherit from the IBM-supplied data area attributes and programs.

For a more detailed description of the object-oriented architecture of the AS/400 system, see the papers in Appendix A.

CHAPTER 10

Object-Oriented Programming Languages

An object-oriented programming language is one that supports and enforces the concepts of objects, classes, and inheritance. In other words, "It provides facilities that make it convenient (reasonably easy, safe, and efficient)" [Stro88] to use those concepts. A surprisingly large number of object-oriented programming languages exist today (one article I read recently reviewed more than 80 different object-oriented languages!), many of which are object-oriented extensions of other languages such as Object Pascal, Object LOGO, and C++. In this chapter, I will give a brief overview of what I consider to be the three most influential of the group: Simula, Smalltalk, and C++.

SIMULA

Simula was designed in the 1960s at the Norwegian Computing Centre by Ole-Johan Dahl and Krysten Nygaard, who required a language for describing and implementing programs that simulated complex, real-time problems. The language name is an abbreviation of "simulation language." Simula extends the ALGOL 60 language, which introduced concepts such as block structure, variable name scoping, type declaration, and recursive subroutines, to include object-oriented extensions such as encapsulation, abstraction, and inheritance. The concepts introduced in Simula influenced the design of almost every subsequent object-based and object-oriented programming language.

The term "object" was introduced as a technical term in Simula to describe the association of data and procedures such that the data would persist across calls to the procedures. Objects were used to represent real-world entities in simulations. The "Simula class" supports the description and declaration of these objects, and subclassing supports inheritance from existing classes; this approach provided a natural way to describe and represent real-world entities and proved very valuable for describing and implementing simulation programs.

The Simula language was known mostly in the simulation area and thus never gained wide acceptance for general development purposes, although it is still in use by a small group in the simulation area. Simula's biggest contribution to programming is the impact it has had on an entirely new generation of programming languages.

Smalltalk

The Smalltalk language was designed in the 1970s by Alan Kay of Xerox corporation, along with Adele Goldberg and Daniel Ingalls, as part of Alan Kay's visionary Dynabook project. Smalltalk was primarily influenced by the object-oriented programming concepts introduced in Simula, and it consists of both a language and a unique programming environment. This unique programming environment forms an intrinsic part of Smalltalk application development.

Smalltalk was designed to trade off implementation efficiency for improved programmer productivity, which it achieves in several ways. Rather than declaring variables with specific types and using type information to statically determine at compile time the appropriate operation to perform, Smalltalk variables are not declared with an associated type. At runtime, the system examines the object to determine its type and dynamically invokes the appropriate routine. For the programmer, this is essentially an abstraction away from the details of type information, which simplifies the use of the variable. A shorter edit-compile-debug cycle is achieved by quickly compiling Smalltalk programs to an interpreter instead of to native hardware. Also, the language handles garbage collection, rather than requiring the programmer to explicitly manage dynamically allocated storage. Smalltalk is considered a pure object-oriented programming language; everything in the language is an object and there is no way to break the defined encapsulation, as is the case with other languages such as C++. Also, you cannot easily mix Smalltalk programs with programs written in other languages, because the environment is fairly self-contained.

"Next to Simula, Smalltalk is perhaps the most important object-oriented programming language, because its concepts have influenced not only the design of almost every subsequent object-oriented programming language, but also the look and feel of graphic user interfaces such as the Macintosh user interface and Motif, which are now largely taken for granted" [Booc91]. The Smalltalk language is fairly popular, particularly on PCs, although it is not yet widely used for application development, partly because of the overhead incurred by the dynamic nature of the language and its supporting environment. It is, however, used quite heavily in teaching object-oriented programming concepts, in much the same way Pascal is used to teach modular programming.

C++

The Smalltalk language is considered by many to be the standard for object-orientation, because of its strict enforcement of object-oriented concepts; but the C++ language, based on the C language, appears to be particularly responsible for the recent increase in the interest in and use of OOP for general software development. A recent survey of the *Communications of the ACM*'s 85,000 readers indicated that of the 36 percent of those responding to the survey who were using object-oriented programming, 83 percent were using C++, with the next highest use (at 10 percent) for Smalltalk. Of the languages (not restricted to object-oriented programming languages) that readers were planning to use, 48 percent of respondents indicated C++. Other than C's planned usage (tallied at 56 percent of respondents), no other language's use was planned by more than 20 percent of the readers responding to the survey[1].

The C++ language was designed in the 1980s by Bjarne Stroustrup of AT&T Bell Laboratories (which is also where the C language originated). Two major design goals for the C++ language were compatibility with the C language and performance. The intention was that C++ programs would run in the same traditional programming environment as C programs, without huge runtime or space inefficiencies. The C++ language extends the ANSI C language with both strong object-oriented programming support and other non-OOP constructs that "clean up" the C language somewhat. The C++ language is considered a separate language from C; but it is almost a complete superset of the ANSI C language, so most ANSI-conforming C programs will be accepted by a C++ compiler. The other major language influence was Simula, from which the class concept and support for inheritance and polymorphism originated.

Because of its strong roots in C, which facilitates the portability of both C programs and C programming skills, C++ is becoming the language of choice for system programming where C has been traditionally used. The C++ language is a natural extension to C, so it is more familiar to C programmers than other OO languages. And because C and C++ code can easily be mixed in one application, allowing C functions to be used with C++ OOP constructs, migration of code from C to C++ can be performed in increments.

[1] The operating system most frequently used by these readers were DOS at 69 percent and UNIX at 55 percent. Sixty-eight percent of the respondents work in industry, 12 percent work for aerospace, defense, or the government, and 20 percent work in education. Of the 81 percent who write, design, or customize software, 47 percent do so for database applications, 42 percent for software tools and utilities, 38 percent for research and development, 32 percent for commercial applications, 31 percent for windows applications, and 31 percent for productivity tools and utilities. Other application areas in which between 5 percent and 20 percent of the respondents were involved include embedded systems, financial systems, AI applications, multimedia applications, and manufacturing process control [ACM91]. Note that since some readers responded positively for multiple categories, the percentages total more than 100 percent.

The remainder of this book provides an introduction to the C++ language. You should find this discussion valuable even if you don't know C and don't plan to use C++, because it will reinforce concepts discussed in the first part of the book through concrete examples based on the OS/400 architecture.

CHAPTER 11

Classes in C++

The C++ support for object-oriented programming is built on the class construct. You define a class using the keyword `class` followed by the class name. The body of the class is enclosed in braces, with a semicolon following the closing brace. Inside the class definition are data and function definitions, which are called *class members*. (A class definition resembles a C structure definition, except that you can declare functions as well as data inside a class.)

In C++, by default, everything defined in a class is hidden; that is, no class member can be referenced outside the class definition. To specify the accessibility of particular class members, you use the *access-specifiers* `private`, `public`, and `protected`. `private`, the default when you specify no access-specifier, means that the member is in the hidden part of the class and can be accessed only by a function defined within the class definition (or a *friend* function, discussed later in Chapter 14). `public` means that the member is in the visible part of the class and, therefore, that any function can access it. In OOP terminology, the public member functions are the methods for that class. I explain the meaning of `protected` when I discuss `derived` *classes* in Chapter 13. An access-specifier applies to all the member definitions following it until the next access-specifier or until the end of the class definition.

The example in Figure 11.1 declares the class `dtaara` with the data member `data` (a pointer to character data, or string, in this context) following the access-specifier `private`, so only functions declared within the class `dtaara` can access `data`. After this declaration comes the access-specifier `public`, followed by four member function declarations — `crtdtaara`, `rtvdtaara`, `chgdtaara`, and `dltdtaara`. Functions in C++ are similar to those in the C language. These four functions are the only functions that can access the data member `data`; no other function in the program can reference or modify it. Because the declarations for these functions follow the access-specifier `public`, functions outside the class definition can call them. In other words, these four member functions are the methods for the class `dtaara`. If any function declaration in Figure 11.1 preceded the keyword `public`, it would be private to the class and could be called only from within the class definition.

The four member functions defined in the class `dtaara` correspond roughly to some of the CL commands that operate on AS/400 DTAARA

FIGURE 11.1
A C++ Class Definition

```
#include <string.h>

class dtaara
{
    private:
        char *data;

    public:
        void crtdtaara(int size)        // create data area
        {
            data = new char[size];
        }

        char *rtvdtaara(void)           // retrieve data
        {
            return data;
        }

        void chgdtaara(char *newdata)   // change data
        {
            strcpy(data, newdata);      // caution: should check lengths
        }

        void dltdtaara(void)           // delete data area
        {
            delete[] data;
        }
};  // end of class dtaara
```

objects. The function `crtdtaara` accepts one parameter — the integer size — and uses the C++ `new` operator to dynamically allocate an array of `size` characters and assign the address of the allocated data to the private class data member `data`. (For those of you familiar with C, `new` is like a typed `malloc`.) The keyword `void` before the function name indicates that `crtdtaara` returns no value. (The // symbols indicate that any text that follows, up to the end of the line, is a comment.)

The function `rtvdtaara` accepts no parameters (indicated by the keyword `void` in parentheses after the function name) and returns a pointer to type `char` (character data). It returns the current value of the string member `data`, corresponding to the storage allocated by `crtdtaara`, if any. The third function, `chgdtaara`, accepts a string called `newdata` and uses the C++ `strcpy` library function to copy the new string value to the member data. (For simplicity, this example performs no error or other checking, but functions such as `chgdtaara` should ensure that the new data fits in the destination before copying it.) Function `dltdtaara` neither accepts any parameters nor returns a value; it simply uses the C++ `delete` operator to de-allocate the storage associated with the member data (the [] used with delete indicate an array is being de-allocated).

Now let's look at how to use this class definition. Figure 11.2 shows a C++ function called main, whose first line is the declaration

```
dtaara my_dtaara;
```

This statement declares the variable my_dtaara, which is of class dtaara. Because dtaara is a class, my_dtaara is not just a simple variable, but an object, consisting of both data and functions, as Figure 11.2 illustrates. When you declare an object, storage is allocated for data members declared within the object's class (in this case, for data). Each declaration of an object of a given class results in a new copy of the storage being allocated, so each object is unique; that is, changing the value of a data member inside one object of a given class does not affect the value of that same data member in a different object of the same class.

The next four lines in Figure 11.2 invoke the member functions for the object my_dtaara. You can invoke a member function using the notation

object.member_function(arguments)

(Those of you familiar with C should recognize this notation as an extension of C structure member access.) This notation invokes the specified function for the object with the given arguments, if any. Note that the member function must be one of those declared as public within the class definition, and you can call those functions only with respect to an object of that class. That is, the member function crtdtaara is not

FIGURE 11.2

Using the dtaara Class

```
#include <iostreams.h>

int main(void)
{
    dtaara my_dtaara;    // declare object of class dtaara

    my_dtaara.crtdtaara(100);    // invoke method crtdtaara
    my_dtaara.chgdtaara("data for the data area");
    cout << "data is: " << my_dtaara.rtvdtaara() << endl;
    my_dtaara.dltdtaara();
}
```

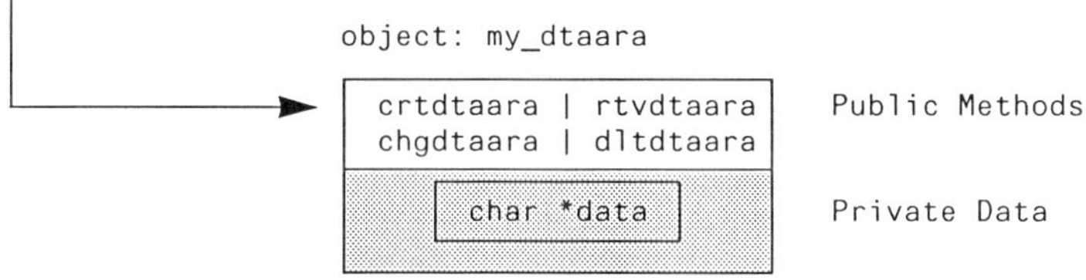

visible except with respect to an object of class `dtaara` and cannot simply be invoked alone. You must invoke the function by giving the object name with which it is associated; otherwise, the compiler issues an error. Likewise, the private member `data` is not visible at all, and you cannot reference it either directly by name or indirectly with respect to an object of class `dtaara`; the compiler will flag such attempts as errors.

The first of the lines after the object declaration in Figure 11.2 invokes the member function (method) `crtdtaara` with a parameter of 100. This causes 100 bytes of storage to be allocated and assigned to the private class member `data`. In OOP terminology, this C++ statement means "Send a message to the object my_dtaara to invoke the method `crtdtaara`"; the arrow in Figure 11.2 represents the message sent. The next line invokes the method `chgdtaara`, passing it a new string value. The third line uses the *stream class operator* `<<` to display the value returned from invoking the method `rtvdtaara`. (A stream in this context is a sequence of characters that is written to the terminal, represented by `cout`. The `<<` operator is similar to a concatenation operator: It formats each operand according to its type and concatenates it to the output data. `endl` is a stream *manipulator* that causes a new output line to be started.) The last line of code in Figure 11.2 invokes the method `dltdtaara`, which deletes the storage allocated by `crtdtaara`.

CHAPTER 12

Using C++ Classes

In Chapter 11 you saw how to declare and use a C++ class. Now let's examine the concept in more detail. The purpose of a class is to group data and associated functions into a logical entity called an object and restrict access to the data and functions through defined interfaces. Note that, as with the AS/400 DTAARA object, the `dtaara` class is defined so that no usage of objects of that class depends on the underlying implementation — because the implementation is hidden inside the class. You could change the internal implementation of the `dtaara` object in a variety of ways without affecting the external usage of that object. Encapsulation isolates changes to the internal class definition from the external interface, as opposed to spreading implementation dependencies throughout the program.

When you invoke a member function for an object, you do not explicitly pass the object itself as a parameter to that function. Rather, the compiler implicitly passes a pointer to the object for which the method was invoked, making the data for a given object available to the member functions. You cannot accidentally invoke a member function with an object for which it was not defined; the compiler will flag such an attempt as an error, reducing both the possibility for error and the amount of error checking required within the member functions themselves.

As an example of this protection, suppose we define a class called `file`. Unless we also explicitly define a public member function for it called `crtdtaara`, we cannot invoke that function against objects of class `file`. You should be getting the impression that a class is a powerful software engineering tool. But wait — there's more!

CONSTRUCTORS AND DESTRUCTORS

The careful readers among you may have noticed that because the methods defined in Chapter 11, Figure 11.1, perform no error handling, invoking a function such as `chgdtaara` before `crtdtaara` would likely result in some kind of error. Given the class definition shown, a complete definition needs to perform error checking to ensure that the caller invokes `crtdtaara` before any of the other methods. Also, the user of the class `dtaara` must be aware of the necessity to invoke both `crtdtaara` to create the data area and `dltdtaara` to delete it.

To reduce the complexity and the possibility for error that such requirements impose, you can define implicit initialization and cleanup routines for C++ classes. Such routines are called *constructors* and *destructors*, respectively. A constructor for a class is called implicitly when an object of that class is created, and the destructor is called implicitly when the object is destroyed. A constructor for a class is a member function with the same name as the class. A destructor has the same name as the class preceded by ~. (The ~ is the C++ *complement operator*; its use here represents a destructor as the complement, or opposite, of a constructor.)

In Figure 12.1a, a constructor and a destructor, respectively, replace the member functions `crtdtaara` and `dltdtaara`. Note that the declaration for the constructor specifies `=200` after the parameter `size`. This provides a default value for the parameter if no argument is passed. Default parameter values let you define functions in a more flexible manner: Instead of forcing the caller to pass all parameters, they permit defaults to be taken.

Figure 12.1a also shows how you can define the member function bodies outside the class definition itself — Figure 12.1b shows these. Keeping class definitions and function bodies separate is important in a development environment: It lets programmers reference the class definitions without seeing (and possibly being influenced by) the implementation details. The compiler directive `#include` (similar to /COPY in RPG) is used to include the class definition from Figure 12.1a in the source in Figure 12.1b. (The include name, `dtaara.h`, uses the Unix file name convention and is equivalent on the AS/400 system to the source member DTAARA in the file H.) The notation `dtaara::` before each function name in Figure 12.1b designates the function as part of the definition for class `dtaara` (so that the compiler recognizes these functions as the member functions corresponding to those specified in the class definition). The

FIGURE 12.1A

Defining a Constructor and a Destructor for Class dtaara

```
source member: dtaara.h

class dtaara
{
    private:
        char *data;

    public:
        dtaara(int size=200);      // constructor for class dtaara
        char *rtvdtaara(void);
        void chgdtaara(char *newdata);
        ~dtaara(void);             // destructor for class dtaara
};
```

FIGURE 12.1B
Class dtaara Member Function Definitions

```
#include <string.h>
#include "dtaara.h"

dtaara::dtaara(int size)       // member function of class dtaara
{
    data = new char[size];
}

char *dtaara::rtvdtaara(void)
{
    return data;
}

void dtaara::chgdtaara(char *newdata)
{
    strcpy(data, newdata);     // caution: should check lengths
}

dtaara::~dtaara(void)
{
    delete[] data;
}
```

definitions for the constructor and destructor functions are identical to those of the `crtdtaara` and `dltdtaara` functions they replace. The constructor allocates storage based on the size given, and the destructor deallocates this storage.

Figure 12.1c illustrates the use of constructors and destructors. Instead of explicitly invoking `crtdtaara` with the number of characters to be allocated, the constructor is implicitly called on the declaration of the object `my_dtaara` and passed the size to allocate. This is similar to declaring an array, where the declaration specifies the array's size,

FIGURE 12.1C
Using a Class with a Constructor and a Destructor Defined

```
#include <iostreams.h>
#include "dtaara.h"

int main(void)
{
    dtaara my_dtaara(100);     // implicitly call dtaara constructor
    dtaara dtaara2;            // implicitly call constructor, default 200

    my_dtaara.chgdtaara("data for the data area");
    cout << "data is: " << my_dtaara.rtvdtaara() << endl;
    // implicitly call destructor for my_dtaara
}
```

although a constructor is much more general in that it is a function that can be passed multiple parameters and perform a variety of operations. The object my_dtaara is destroyed when the function containing it ends, so when the function main ends, the destructor for my_dtaara is implicitly called, replacing the explicit invocation of dltdtaara. The declaration of the dtaara object dtaara2 shows how to use the default value specified on the constructor definition. Because no parameter is passed, the compiler assigns a default value of 200 to size; this declaration results in the constructor being called and allocating 200 bytes for the object dtaara2.

Note how much simpler the use of constructors and destructors makes the code on both sides. On the class definition side, the member functions can assume that certain initialization steps have already taken place, reducing error-checking requirements and simplifying the coding effort. On the class usage side, the user of the class need no longer perform explicit initialization and cleanup for an object.

Operator Overloading

Invoking member functions by name isn't always the most convenient way to access object functionality. If you think of an object as a variable, you often want to perform common operations such as addition and subtraction, just as you would with simple C++ variables (e.g., using + and - operators). For example, adding a fixed number of days to a date object is more naturally coded as

```
date2 = date1 + 15
```

rather than

```
date2 = inc_date(date1, 15)
```

C++ lets you overload operators such as + and = for use with objects. Based on the type and the number of operands being operated on, the compiler selects the appropriate processing routine for the operator.

Figure 12.2a shows the partial definition of a class called date. This class has three private data members used to represent the value of a date object: the integers day, month, and year. In the public portion of the class is an incomplete list of member functions. Note that there are two constructors (both named date): one with no parameters and one with three. Based on how an object of class date is defined (with no initial value or with three integer initial values), the compiler picks the appropriate constructor to call. (This is an example of function overloading.)

The final member function in the list is defined using the keyword operator followed by =. This statement defines a function to be called when the = operator is applied against a date object with another date

FIGURE 12.2A
Partial Definition for the Class `date`

```
class date
{
    private:
        int day;
        int month;
        int year;

    public:
        date();                                  // constructor
        date(int dd, int mm, int yy);            // constructor
        void set_date(int dd, int mm, int yy);
        void operator=(date from_date);
        .
        .
        .
};
```

object on the right-hand side of the `=`. The `date` object from which the assignment is being made is the parameter for this function.

Figure 12.2b shows the full definitions for the member functions specified in Figure 12.2a. When a program applies the `=` operator to a `date` object, the final member function in Figure 12.2b will be called to copy the value of the `date` object `from_date` to the current object. Note that because `from_date` is also a `date`, member functions for the class `date` can access this object's private data. The concept of private members is enforced at a class level, not at an individual object level.

Given that `date1` and `date2` are objects of class `date`, you could then write

```
date1 = date2;
```

to assign the value of `date2` to `date1`. You could write this equivalently as

```
date1.operator=(date2);
```

This statement shows how the compiler interprets the `=` operator: The member function `operator=` is called and is passed the parameter `date2`. Note that this example defines `=` only for a `date` object on the right-hand side of the `= operator`. If `date2` were some other type (e.g., an integer), the compiler would issue an error because no matching member function definition exists for this combination. You could, however, define another version of the `operator=` function that accepted a different variable type as the parameter, and the compiler would select the appropriate routine to call based on the parameter type.

Operator overloading substantially increases code readability, and it simplifies the programmer's job because there are fewer new things to

FIGURE 12.2B
Overloading Operators

```
date::date()
{
    day = 0;
    month = 0;
    year = 0;
}


date::date(int dd, int mm, int yy)
{
    day = dd;
    month = mm;
    year = yy;
}


void date::set_date(int dd, int mm, int yy)
{
    day = dd;
    month = mm;
    year = yy;
}


void date::operator=(date from_date)
{
    day = from_date.day;
    month = from_date.month;
    year = from_date.year;
}
```

learn. Instead of remembering a new function name (e.g., `assign`), you can take advantage of the `=` operator's readily recognized and understood meaning. Figure 12.3 shows the definition of a class `employee` that uses objects of class `date`. An `employee` object contains a name, number, hire date, and date when the employee is eligible for benefits. This example shows how you can declare a class object data member (e.g., `date_hired`, which is itself an object) inside a class definition the same way you declare simple data members (e.g., the pointer `name` or the integer `emp_num`). Again, though, the only way to operate on such data members is through their public class members. The constructor for an `employee` object initializes `name` and `emp_num` explicitly and then implicitly calls the constructors for the `date` objects `date_hired` and `date_for_benefits` (using the `date` constructor with no parameters).

The member function `set_hire_date` accepts a `date` object, `hire_date`, as a parameter. The first line of that function uses the overloaded `= operator` to assign `hire_date` to the private object `date_hired`. Assuming an employee is eligible for benefits 90 days after

FIGURE 12.3

Using Operator Overloading

```
#include <string.h>
#include "datecls.h"

class employee
{
    private:
        char *name;
        int emp_num;
        date date_hired, date_for_benefits;      // call date constructor

    public:
        employee(void)
        {
            name = NULL;
            emp_num = 0;
            // date constructor for dates called implicitly
        }

        ~employee(void)
        {
            if (name != NULL)
                delete[] name;
        }

        void set_name(char *emp_name)
        {
            name = new char[strlen(emp_name) + 1];
            strcpy(name, emp_name);
        }

        void set_hire_date(date hire_date)
        {
            date_hired = hire_date;
            date_for_benefits = hire_date + 90;     // overload +
        }

        date hire_date(void)
        {
            return(date_hired);
        }
};

void main(void)
{
    employee emp;

    emp.set_name("Arthur Dent");
    emp.set_hire_date(date(23, 10, 90));
    if (emp.hire_date() < date(01, 01, 91))             // overload <
        cout << "Employee hired: " << emp.hire_date();  // overload <<
}
```

the hire date, the next statement reflects this by adding 90 to `hire_date` and assigning the result to `date_for_benefits`. This statement uses both the overloaded `=` and `+` operators (you would define the overload for `+` with a date in a similar fashion to `=`). Note how readable the statement is: Its intention is obvious, requiring little interpretation.

The `main` function at the bottom of Figure 12.3 shows how you might use an employee object. The first line of code declares the object `emp` and is followed by the invocation of the member function `set_name` to set the employees name. The next line sets the hire date, using an explicit call to the `date` class constructor to construct from the passed parameters a date, which is then passed to `set_hire_date`. (Calling the date constructor is similar to calling a conversion routine to convert an integer to a floating-point number before passing it to a function that accepts such a parameter.) The final `if` statement uses an overload of the < operator to compare two date values, again using an explicit call to the date constructor and then displaying the `date` value using an overload of the stream class operator `<<`. This final overload might format the `date` value using separators (e.g., `'/'`) and return the formatted string, which would be concatenated to the output stream.

CHAPTER 13

Derived Classes in C++

By themselves, C++'s concept of and support for classes provide an enormous improvement over traditional high-level languages in isolating and grouping data and the routines that operate on that data. Inheritance, which was discussed in Chapter 7, augments this support by letting you create a new class and base it on an existing class definition. This ability is supported in C++ through the concept of *derived classes.*

A derived class includes a copy of all the data members of the base class, plus its own data and functions. In its simplest form, you define a derived class as shown in Figure 13.1. The access-specifier can be either `public`, `private`, or `protected` as follows:

- `public`: Public members in the base class are public in the derived class, and protected members in the base class are protected in the derived class.
- `private`: Public and protected members in the base class are private in the derived class.
- `protected`: Public and protected (still to be covered) members in the base class are protected in the derived class.

Private members in the base class are always private and cannot be directly referenced in the derived class. The derived class can access the copy of private data it received from the base class only through the member functions for the base class.

Figure 13.2 shows a sample base class called `base_class` used by the derived class `dtaara`. `base_class` has three private data members — the name, library, and owner of the object — and two public member functions, `crtobj` and `dspobjd`. (`base_class` is modeled after the common attributes belonging to all AS/400 system objects.)

The class `dtaara` derives from `base_class` using the access-specifier

FIGURE 13.1
Syntax for Defining a Derived Class

```
class derived_class_name: access-specifier base_class_name
{
    // class body
}
```

FIGURE 13.2
A Simple Derived Class

```
#include <iostreams.h>
#include <string.h>

class base_class
{
    private:
        char name[11];
        char library[11];
        char owner[11];


    public:
        void crtobj(char *obj_name, char *obj_library)
        {
            strcpy(name, obj_name);
            strcpy(library, obj_library);
            strcpy(owner, "jennifer");
        }


        void dspobjd(void)
        {
            cout << "name: " << name << endl << "lib: " << library;
            cout << endl << "owner: " << owner;
        }
};


class dtaara : public base_class
{
    private:
        char *data;

    public:
        void crtdtaara(char *name, char *library, int size)
        {
            data = new char[size];
            crtobj(name, library);  // implicit access to base data
        }
};


void main(void)
{
    dtaara my_dtaara;

    my_dtaara.crtdtaara("dtaara1", "mylib", 100);
    my_dtaara.dspobjd();  // member function from base class
}
```

`public`, so it inherits and can access the two public members of `base_class`. I've extended the definition for the `crtdtaara` method to assign object attributes by calling function `crtobj`, as well as to allocate storage. Note that this use of `crtobj` does not require an object name to be specified with it; the member function is called directly. Because the `dtaara` class is derived from `base_class`, each `dtaara` object contains a copy of the `base_class` data, and calling `crtobj` as such invokes it for the `base_class` data contained in the current object (i.e., an object of class `dtaara`). You cannot explicitly reference the data in `base_class`, however, because it is private to that class.

Not only is any `base_class` data implicitly part of a `dtaara` object, but the public functions of `base_class` can also be applied to `dtaara` objects. The last line of the `main` function in Figure 13.2 can use the function `dspobjd` with the `dtaara` object `my_dtaara` because the `dtaara` class *inherits* the functions and data of `base_class`. The concept of inheritance in object-oriented languages (OOLs) lets you write software in such a way that it can naturally be reused and extended. For example, we could add a new public function to `base_class` (e.g., `movobj`), and with no code changes to `dtaara` objects, we could also apply this function to `dtaara` objects. This ease of extendibility is one of the most powerful of the OOP advantages over traditional programming methodologies.

PROTECTED CLASS MEMBERS

Note that given the class definitions in Figure 13.2, a program can directly apply the `crtobj` function to objects of class `dtaara`. If we were designing a system that followed the AS/400 system object model, we would not want `crtobj` to be used that way. `crtdtaara` should be used to create the `dtaara` object, a step that in turn would call `crtobj`; but crtobj should not be directly callable with `dtaara` objects. We want `crtobj` visible within the `dtaara` class, but not outside it. Simply making `crtobj` private in `base_class` would not achieve this because then it could not be called from `crtdtaara`. The way to achieve our objective in C++ is by using the access-specifier `protected`.

`protected` means that only a function within the class definition or within a class derived from that class (or a `friend` function of either the base or derived class) can access the member. Figure 13.3 shows the example from Figure 13.2, using `protected` ahead of `crtobj`. The rest of the example remains the same, but the key difference is that any attempt to use `crtobj` with a `dtaara` object will result in a compiler error because `crtobj` is not visible outside the derived class `dtaara`.

MULTIPLE INHERITANCE

C++ supports multiple inheritance by allowing a derived class to inherit from more than one base class. The syntax, shown in Figure 13.4, is an extension to that of single inheritance. You can precede any base class name with the access-specifier `private`, `protected`, or `public`. If you use no access-specifier, the default is `private`. For a simple example, consider the class `save_file` shown in Figure 13.5. This class is derived from class `file` as a public base class and from class `space` as a private base class.

FIGURE 13.3
Using the Access-Specifier protected

```
#include <iostreams.h>
#include <string.h>


class base_class
{
    private:
        char name[11];
        char library[11];
        char owner[11];

    protected:
        void crtobj(char *obj_name, char *obj_library)
        {
            strcpy(name, obj_name);
            strcpy(library, obj_library);
            strcpy(owner, "jennifer");
        }

    public:
        void dspobjd(void)
        {
            cout << "name: " << name << endl << "lib: " << library;
            cout << endl << "owner: " << owner;
        }
};


class dtaara : public base_class
              .
              .
              .
```

FIGURE 13.4
Syntax for Defining a Derived Class with Multiple Inheritance

```
class derived_class_name: access-specifier base_class1, access-specifier
   base_class2, ...
{
    // class body
}
```

FIGURE 13.5
Multiple Inheritance

```
class space {
};

class file {
};

class save_file : public file, private space
{
};
```

CHAPTER 14

Additional C++ Constructs

Isolating and protecting data access through classes provides a great deal of protection against software problems. On occasion, however, the overhead of such protection is unacceptable. When you make many references to an object, the overhead of a function call for each access can detrimentally affect system performance. The ability to directly access the data from outside the class, although it breaks the object model, is sometimes required for performance-sensitive applications. You can achieve such access in a controlled fashion using the C++ `friend` specifier.

THE `friend` SPECIFIER

The `friend` specifier lets you define a function or an entire class as a *friend* of another class. Then that function, or all the functions within the friend class, gains access to the private members of the given class as if it (or they) were part of the class. You should use the `friend` specifier only where absolutely needed: Use it too much, and you lose the advantages of an object-oriented approach.

Another use of the `friend` specifier is in migrating applications from C to C++. To ease the conversion, you could define all data as private to a class but make the C functions that access that data friends of the class. Ultimately, you'd want to make those C functions class members or to write them to use the appropriate class interfaces.

Figure 14.1 shows a sample class called `simple`, where the class `other_class` and the function `show_value` are declared as friends of the class. Any member function in the class `other_class`, along with the function `show_value`, can access the private data of the class `simple`. The example defines only the function `show_value`; this function accepts one parameter, an object of class `simple`, and then directly accesses the object's private data member, `number`, to display the value. The code in the `main` function shows the difference between invoking a class member function against an object and simply calling a function. `set_value` is a class member function of the class `simple` and must be called with respect to an object of that class; the object data is implicitly available to that function. `show_value`, on the other hand, is called directly from the `main` function through a standard function call, and the object is passed explicitly as an argument to that function.

FIGURE 14.1
Using the friend Specifier

```
#include <iostreams.h>

class simple
{
    private:
        int number;

    public:
        void set_value(int newval) { number = newval; }
        friend class other_class;
        friend void show_value(simple obj);
};

void show_value(simple obj)
{
    cout << "value is: " << obj.number << endl;
}

void main(void)
{
    simple obj;

    obj.set_value(6);
    show_value(obj);
}
```

VIRTUAL FUNCTIONS

All of the C++ examples so far have used static binding, which is the default binding for the C++ language. There is support for polymorphism and dynamic binding, however, through *virtual functions.* A virtual function is resolved at runtime, based on the target object type, or *runtime type,* rather than at compile time. You define a function as virtual by specifying the keyword `virtual` in front of a member function for a base class. Each derived class can then either supply its own version of that function or use that defined in the parent class. When a virtual method is invoked against a pointer to some subclass of the original base class, the appropriate member function is called according to the runtime object type.

As an example, Figure 14.2a shows the definition of a base class called `file` with a virtual member function called `display_file_descrip`. Three classes are derived from this class: `display_file`, `save_file`, and `simple_file`, the first two of which supply their own versions of the member function `display_file_descrip`. A definition supplied in a derived class for a virtual function in the base class is itself virtual. You can include the keyword `virtual` in front of the derived class member function, but it is redundant. Figure 14.2b shows the output from the program.

Figure 14.2a
Defining a Virtual Function

```
#include <iostream.h>

class file
{
    public:
        virtual void display_file_descrip(void)
        {
            cout << "file description" << endl;
        }
};


class display_file : public file
{
    public:
        void display_file_descrip(void)
        {
            cout << "display_file description" << endl;
        }
};


class save_file : public file
{
    public:
        void display_file_descrip(void)
        {
            cout << "save_file description" << endl;
        }
};

class simple_file: public file
{
};


int main(void)
{
    file *file1;
    display_file dspf1;
    save_file savf1;
    simple_file simple1;

    file1 = &dspf1;
    file1->display_file_descrip();
    file1 = &savf1;
    file1->display_file_descrip();
    file1 = &simple1;
    file1->display_file_descrip();
}
```

FIGURE 14.2b
Program Output

```
display_file description
save_file description
file description
```

In the main function for the program, a pointer to a file object, file1, is declared, along with three objects, dspf1, savf1, and simple1. The program then sets file1 to point to dspf1 and invokes the display_file_descrip member function (using the -> operator to invoke a method for an object that is pointed to).

Because that member function was defined as virtual in the base class, the member function to be invoked is not determined until runtime. In this case, the runtime type of the object is display_file, so the display_file_descrip member function for the display_file class will be invoked. The message displayed will be "display_file description". If that member function were not declared as virtual, the member function for the file class would be called when display_file_descrip was invoked against file1, because at compile time the compiler would determine the type of the object being pointed to; in this case, file1 is defined to point to objects of type file and create a static link to the member function for the file class.

The next two lines set file1 to point to savf1 and then invoke the display_file_descrip method against file1 once more. This time, file1 will be pointing to an object of the save_file class, so the display_file_descrip member function for that class will be called, resulting in the message "save_file description". The final two lines set file1 to point to simple1, again invoking the member function. This time, because the class simple did not provide a definition for display_file_descrip, the member function in the base class file is used, so the message displayed will be "file description".

ADDITIONAL OOP SUPPORT

In the last four chapters, I have attempted to cover only the main aspects of C++'s support for object-oriented programming. The language has additional OOP features, including the stream class library, templates, and exception handling. The stream class library supports stream I/O in an object-oriented fashion; I have shown you a couple of examples of using the stream class operator <<. Templates let you define classes independent of type, so that the data type to be operated on is essentially a parameter to the class definition at compile time. (The Ada language's concept of generics is similar.) C++ exception-handling support is also object-oriented and provides powerful error-handling capabilities.

Learning C++

Although no C++ compiler is available on the AS/400 system, many AS/400 programmers are purchasing C++ compilers for their PCs. I frequently am asked whether it is necessary to learn C before learning C++. My answer is that it depends upon the background of the programmer. But, because C++ is a superset of C, learning C first will certainly not be a waste of time, as almost anything you learn about C can be applied to C++.

If your main programming language experience is with languages such as RPG or COBOL, you are well-advised to learn the basics of the C language before tackling C++. I have spoken with several RPG programmers who went straight from RPG to C++ and, in retrospect, felt that learning C first would have made the learning process substantially easier. Although most C++ books cover the language completely, including the C subset, such books typically assume a background that the average RPG or COBOL programmer doesn't have (such as an understanding of the concepts of local variables, automatic storage, and recursion).

If you are coming from a language such as Pascal or PL/I, and you want to learn the language for mostly educational purposes, you can probably go straight to C++ with this background. However, if you plan to do any serious programming in C++, you would likely benefit from learning C first. "The trouble is that if you set out to learn C++, you will probably be in a place where people take … C knowledge for granted" [Koen93]. There are several unique features and programming practices of the C language that need to be understood to program effectively in C++, and most C++ books do not cover them in much detail.

I hope this introduction has given you a good start for learning the C++ language. If you want to learn more about object-oriented programming and C++, turn to the references listed in the "Afterword."

Afterword

You should now be familiar with the basic object-oriented programming concepts and their importance in improving how we design and develop software. Object-oriented programming can help us to control software complexity and provide greater software reusability, extensibility, and reliability, with decreased development and maintenance costs.

Now that you have an answer to the question "What is object-oriented programming?", the next question is "Where do you go from here?". One perfectly reasonable choice would be to simply consider this book educational and not pursue the topic any further. I have only attempted to cover the basic concepts at a level of detail sufficient to give you an understanding of the fundamentals, but I purposely did not go into an overwhelming level of detail.

If you do want to go further, however, the next step would be to learn more about the topic. Many journals, books, and papers have been written on the topic of object-oriented programming, with more arriving daily!

Along with the recommended reading below, several journals are devoted specifically to object-oriented programming and OO programming languages, including *Journal of Object-Oriented Programming*, *Object Magazine*, *OOPS Messenger*, *The C++ Journal*, the *C++ Report*, and *The Smalltalk Report*. See "A Quick Look at Computer Language Magazines" by Chuck Lundgren in the September 1992 issue of *NEWS 3X/400* for detailed overviews of these and other journals specific to programming languages. I regularly read *Journal of Object-Oriented Programming* and find it to be an educational magazine that covers a wide variety of topics.

To learn more about the software crisis and the problems that face software developers, see Dijkstra's "The Humble Programmer" [Dijk71] and "No Silver Bullet: Essence and Accidents in Software Engineering" [Broo87] by Brooks. Both are entertaining and informative papers, written in a fairly informal style.

The concepts of information hiding and modular decomposition were introduced by Parnas in "A Technique for Software Module Specification with Examples" [Parn72a] and "On the Criteria to be Used in Decomposing Systems into Modules" [Parn72b], both of which provide excellent and very readable discussion of those topics.

Abstract data types were introduced by Liskov and Zilles in "Programming with Abstract Data Types" [LZ80]. This paper covers the topic well, as does *Abstraction and Specification in Program Development* [LG86], which also covers procedural abstraction and abstraction in general. For a good example of implementing abstract data types in RPG, see "The Last Date Routines You'll Ever Need," March, April, May, and June 1990, *NEWS 3X/400* magazine, and "Screen Input by the Numbers," March 1993, *NEWS 3X/400* magazine.

Classics in Software Engineering [Your79] is a good collection of influential papers in the field of software engineering, including two of the above papers by Dijkstra and Parnas [Parn72a] and many others, such as "Go To Statement Considered Harmful" by Dijkstra; "Programming Style: Examples and Counterexamples" by B. Kernighan and P. Plauger; and "Structured Design" by W. Stevens, G. Myers, and L. Constantine. Yourdon's editorial introductions to each paper are also very informative. A companion book, *Writings of the Revolution: Selected Readings on Software Engineering* [Your82] contains the other aforementioned paper by Parnas [Parn72b], and others such as "Program Development by Stepwise Refinement" by N. Wirth and "The Magical Number Seven, Plus or Minus Two: Some Limits on Our Capacity for Processing Information" by G. A. Miller.

In "What is Object-Oriented Programming?" [Stro88], Stroustrup, the designer of the C++ language, discusses several programming techniques, such as information hiding and abstract data types, contrasting language support, and enablement of these concepts. Most of this paper is reproduced in sections 1.2, 1.4, 1.5, and 1.6 of *The C++ Language* [Stro91].

"An Object-Oriented Tower of Babel" [Nels91] provides a clear explanation of OOP concepts and terminology in a shorter and slightly less academic form than "Dimensions of Object-Based Language Design" [Wegn87], which is a heavily referenced and relatively readable paper that provides definitive explanations of many object-oriented programming concepts. "The Essence of Objects: Concepts and Terms" [Snyd93] defines the core, unifying concepts of the object model across the many types of object systems.

For a more detailed discussion and comparison of the operator/operand and message/object models, see Cox's "Message/Object Programming: An Evolutionary Change in Programming Technology" [Cox84].

Object-Oriented Computing is a two-volume collection of papers related to object-oriented computing. *Volume 1: Concepts* [Pete90] is more generally interesting, containing papers such as Rentsch's "Object-Oriented Programming" [Rent82], "Object-Oriented Software Systems" by Robson [Robs81], "Message/Object Programming: An Evolutionary Approach" by Cox [Cox84], and "Object-Oriented Programming: Themes and Variations" by Stefik and Bobrow [SB86]. *Volume 2: Implementations* [Pete87] includes

"Design Considerations for the IBM System/38" by F. Soltis and R. Hoffman, "Object-Oriented Development" by G. Booch, "Reusability: The Case for Object-Oriented Design" by B. Meyer, "Abstraction Techniques in Modern Programming Languages" by Shaw [Shaw84], and "The Modular Structure of Complex Systems" [PCW85] by Parnas et. al.

Object-Oriented Design with Applications [Booc91], provides a good discussion of the history behind object-oriented programming and the concepts that make up the object model, along with very detailed coverage of both object-oriented design and programming. This book is becoming standard reading in the field of object-oriented computing and is also an excellent source of reference information. Pages 105-108 of this book also provide a good explanation and comparison of the dynamic binding implementation and overhead of the Smalltalk and C++ languages.

Object-Oriented Technology: A Manager's Guide [Tayl90] discusses the history, goals, and concepts of object-oriented technology in general (including databases, user interfaces, etc.) at a fairly high level. It is a relatively small and accessible book.

In "What to you do after you say 'Hello World'?" [Koen93], Keonig gives good, practical advice on how to approach learning C++. If you do want to learn the C language first, RPG programmers should refer to *C for RPG Programmers* (Hamilton, J. Loveland, CO: Duke Press, 1992). Two other good sources of information are *The C Programming Language* 2nd ed. (Kernighan, B. and Ritchie, D. Englewood Cliffs, NJ: Prentice-Hall, 1988), which is the bible for most C programmers, and *C Traps and Pitfalls* (Koenig, A. Reading, MA: Addison-Wesley, 1989), which will help you understand and avoid many common errors, and will also give you a deeper understanding of the C language.

An Introduction to Object-Oriented Programming and C++ [WP88] provides a straightforward introduction to OOP and C++. This book does not cover some of the more recent enhancements to the language, such as templates and exceptions, but it is a very good introductory book, particularly if you don't know C or don't have much background with OOP.

Class Construction in C and C++ [Sess92] provides a very readable and interesting discussion of object-oriented programming concepts and how to implement them first in C and then in C++. It assumes that the reader is somewhat familiar with the C language, and builds on a series of examples that illustrate the value of object-oriented programming and the need for language support.

The C++ Programming Language [Stro91] covers all the details of C++ but is fairly heavy reading unless you are already familiar with C and OOP concepts. If you are, though, I recommend this book — it covers the language completely and provides a lot of insight into language design and usage considerations. Another good C++ book is *The C++ Primer* 2nd ed. (Lippman, S. Reading, MA: Addison-Wesley, 1991). Although I haven't had a chance to read it yet, many people have recommended it.

For detailed information to help you locate these and additional sources, refer to "References" on page 105.

Assuming you want to start using what you've learned, you can take several approaches. If you don't have access to an object-oriented programming language, you can still use many of the concepts covered with languages such as RPG and COBOL. You can apply the principles of abstraction and encapsulation to design your systems using an object-based approach, as discussed in Chapter 5. The OS/400 operating system is a good example of an object-based application that is not written in an object-oriented programming language. The next step would be to experiment with object-oriented programming languages (of which there are a multitude available for PC-based operating systems), such as C++ or Smalltalk. Or you can go even further and start developing production applications using one of these languages.

The choice is up to you. I hope this book has provided you with an important first step to understanding and appreciating object-oriented programming.

Appendix A

The Object-Oriented Architecture of the AS/400 System

This appendix contains reprints of three papers from *IBM System/38 Technical Developments*[1], which was published in 1978 when the S/38 system was introduced and is now long out of print. The papers provide valuable insight into the design goals and object-oriented architecture of the S/38 system, which are embodied in its successor, the AS/400 system.

Through describing the system architecture in terms of encapsulation and objects, the papers emphasize the point made in Chapter 1 that object-oriented concepts are not new. The meanings attributed to these terms in 1978 are basically the same today. The papers also provide fairly compelling evidence that when people refer to the AS/400 system as being object-oriented or object-based, they are not simply jumping on the object-oriented bandwagon. The system was designed with object-oriented concepts in mind from the beginning and incorporates the concepts extensively.

[1] Copyright ©1978 by IBM Corporation, White PLains, NY. IBM G580-0237. Reprinted with permission.

SYSTEM/38 — A HIGH-LEVEL MACHINE

Characterizes the System/38 high-level machine instruction interface. Describes microcoded functions and the rationale for providing them.

by S.H. Dahlby, G.G. Henry, D.N. Reynolds, and P.T. Taylor

One of the primary characteristics of the IBM System/38 that identifies it as an advanced computer system is its high-level machine instruction interface, which incorporates new architectural structures and provides a much higher level of function than traditional machine architectures, such as the IBM System/3. The function and architectural structures are more similar to those of high-level languages than to conventional machines. The purpose of this article is to describe the advantages and salient architectural features provided by the System/38 instruction interface, and how they are realized in the specifics of the System/38 machine.

Relevant System Objectives

Many factors influence the choice of the architectural characteristics [Henr78] of a new system. In System/38 the primary influences, such as anticipated user requirements and hardware technology trends, led to the adoption of some major objectives for the total system. Briefly, these were:

- Programming independence from machine implementation and configuration details
- High levels of integrity and authorization capability with minimal overhead
- Efficient support in the machine for commonly used operations in control programming, compilers, and utilities
- Efficient support in the machine for key system functional objectives, such as data base and dynamic multiprogramming.

The following sections highlight the major System/38 instruction interface concepts and features that address these objectives.

Independence from Machine Implementation and Configuration

In previous systems, the ability for users to take advantage of new technology and implement new function was limited by dependence on a specific low-level instruction interface; for example, dependence upon the hardware-implemented address size. One of the major goals of System/38 architecture was to enable users to be as independent as possible of hardware and device characteristics.

In System/38, hardware dependencies have been absorbed by internal microcode functions that provide an instruction interface, which is largely independent of hardware details. Users of the instruction interface, therefore, need not be concerned with hardware addressing [BTR78], auxiliary storage allocation and addressing [FCL78], internal data structures and relationships [PRM78], channel and I/O interface details, and internal microprogramming details [HS78].

This hardware independence characteristic of the System/38 instruction interface is due in large measure to the use of an object-oriented interface [PRM78] instead of the more conventional byte-oriented interface. An *object* is a System/38 instruction interface construct that contains a specific type of information and can be used only in a specific manner. A number of different types of objects are defined in the interface, and various object-specific instructions are provided to operate upon each object type. An example of a System/38 instruction interface object is a data space (file), which has associated instructions for operations such as the adding and deleting of records [WA78].

Each object is created by a System/38 interface instruction that uses a user-specified data structure to define the object's characteristics and initial values. Once the object is created, its internal stored format is not apparent to the user (with the one exception discussed below). The status and values of the object may be retrieved or changed by using interface instructions, but the internal format of the object cannot be directly viewed or modified. That is, objects can be operated upon functionally, but not as a byte string. This approach prevents dependence on the internal format of the object and enables applications to remain independent of evolving internal implementations of the machine.

There is one specific exception to this shielding of the internal format of an object. A *space object* is a construct that can be used by a program for storage of and operation upon byte-oriented operands such as character strings and numeric values.

In addition to this object orientation, main storage and auxiliary storage addresses are not directly apparent in the System/38 instruction interface [BTR78, PRM78]. All interface addressing of objects is accomplished by resolving symbolic names (supplied by the user) to a pointer. A *pointer* is an object that is used only for addressing and does not permit examination or manipulation of the implied physical address. A *system pointer* gives a user the ability to address objects; for example, to create or destroy an object or to examine or directly modify its content through associated specific instructions. A *space pointer* allows the direct addressability of bytes within a space object. Both of these pointer types can be contained within a space object, but they can be used for addressing only when operated on by pointer manipulation instructions. Pointers are assured of validity via tagged storage in both main and secondary storage. Direct modification of a pointer area via a computational instruction results in the tag becoming invalid and causes the pointer to no longer be usable for addressing purposes.

Similarly, users are not concerned with the addressing structures of either main storage or auxiliary storage [FCL78], or even necessarily that there are multiple levels of storage, since all storage used for all objects in the system is allocated and managed by the machine. That is, there is no differentiation in the System/38 instruction interface as to where an object or portions of an object reside. The total address space of *System/38* thus consists of an unconstrained number of objects, uniformly addressable by pointers.

Similar constructs shield the System/38 instruction interface user from dependencies upon channel and I/O device addresses and low-level communication protocols.

Figure 1 illustrates this basic object-oriented, high-level interface approach.

FIGURE 1
System/38 Object-Oriented Structure

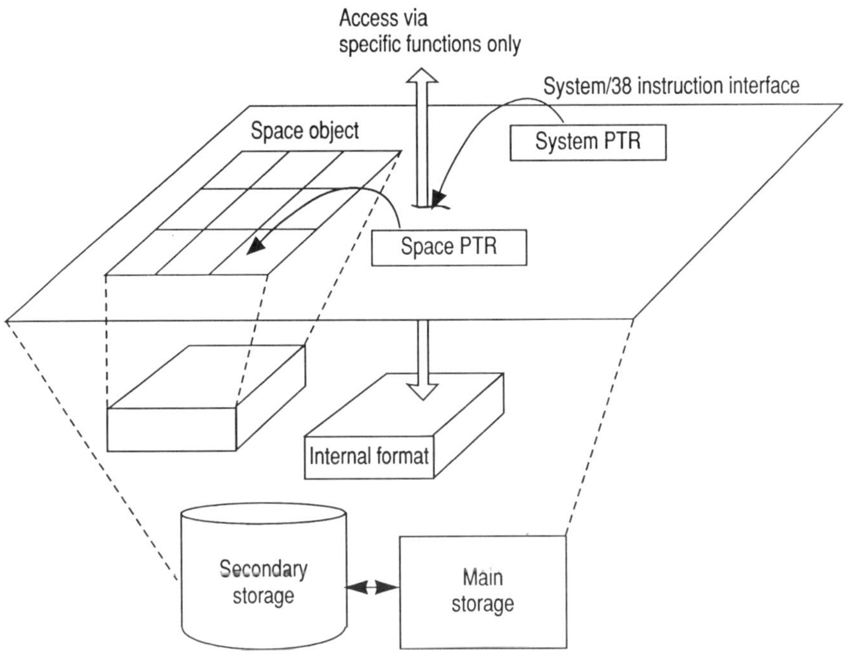

Integrity and Authorization

A natural consequence of the object-oriented approach is improved system integrity and authorization mechanisms [BTR78]. All user information is stored in System/38 instruction interface objects. Access to that information is through System/38 instructions that ensure the structural integrity of the manipulated objects. An attempt to misuse an object is thus detected and causes the instruction execution to be terminated and an exception condition to be raised. An example is the attempt to directly change a byte within a program object.

Authorization capabilities are likewise facilitated by the System/38 instruction-interface object-oriented structure. Each user of the machine is identified by a user profile, which is itself an object. Each object in the system is owned by a user profile, and the owner may delegate to other user profiles various types of authority to operate on the objects. Processes (tasks) execute under a specific user profile (in the name of a user), and functions executed within a process verify that the objects referenced have been properly authorized to that user.

Figure 2 illustrates this approach to providing integrity and authorization capability.

FIGURE 2

System/38 Instruction Interface Integrity and Authorization Scheme

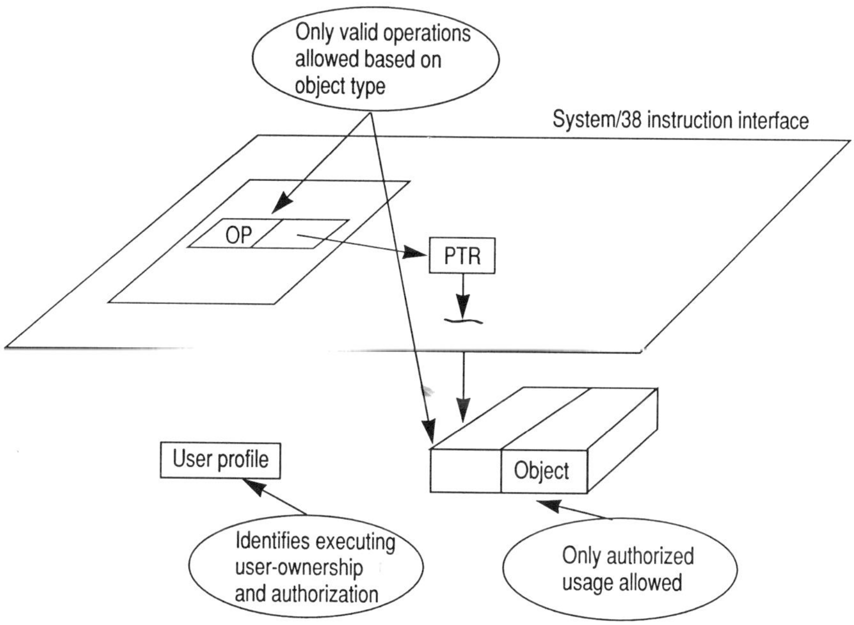

Support for Common Programming Functions

The System/38 instruction interface is designed to provide direct support for a wide variety of functions common to control programming, compilers, and utilities. This increased level of machine function eliminates the need to implement these common functions in multiple programming components, increases consistency across all programming components, and supports programming approaches conducive to providing integrity and reliability.

There are two basic modes of addressing in the System/38 interface. The first is *pointers*, which allow varying addressability to all objects and bytes within space objects. The second, *dictionary addressing*, deals with program references *to* values within a space object.

Operands referenced in program instructions are defined in a dictionary portion of the program separate from the instructions themselves. Instruction operands are index references to these dictionary entries which define operand characteristics such as data type and length. Binary, zoned decimal, packed decimal, character, and pointer data types are examples of operand characteristics that may be defined. The dictionary entries do not contain the operand values; the specific location of the operands is not apparent to or required by programs. However, the user can control the general type of location characteristics: for example, relative to the area addressed by a pointer or relative to the storage area allocated for program variables within the executing process.

This approach of having instructions reference dictionary entries describing the operand characteristics allows additional capability over low-level instruction interfaces. For example, the following high-level capabilities are provided:

- Computational instructions are generic with respect to data type and length. For example, there is only one numeric add instruction in the System/38 instruction interface; it operates on whatever data is defined in the operand definition dictionary. This enables the use of source and receiver operands of varying type, length, and decimal positioning with all conversions and scaling being performed by the machine.
- Arrays may be defined in the interface and instruction operands support array indexing to locate specific elements of the array.
- Since applications often allow operations on multiple formats of data, some instructions (for example, the copy instructions) support late binding of data definition where the data (type, length, and decimal positioning) need not be defined until the instruction is executed.

In addition to these types of high-level data operations, the System/38 instruction interface provides and, in some cases, requires functions intended to support programming constructs more directly than in traditional machines. For example, programs are invoked through call/return functions defined in the interface. Argument/parameter functions provide communications from one program to another. Allocation and initialization of storage for program variables within a process is performed by the System/38 machine. Additional examples are found in Watson [WA78] and Howard [HB78].

Figure 3 illustrates this System/38 program structure and the general relationship between a high-level language program and the corresponding System/38 constructs.

Support for Key System Functions

The System/38 machine was designed to support a usage environment characterized by a dynamically changing application load consisting of a wide variety of application types — all utilizing advanced functions such as data base. For example, batch, interactive, and transaction processing,

FIGURE 3
System/38 Instruction Interface Program Structure

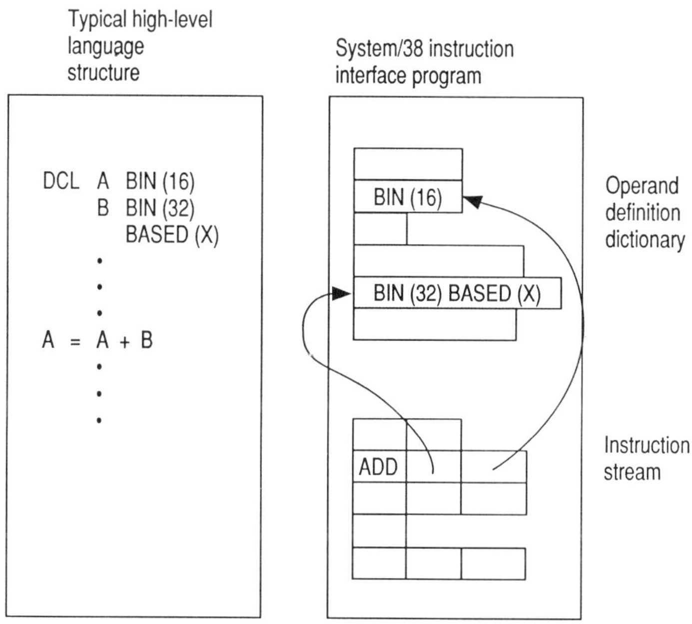

along with program development activities, may all be executing concurrently with dynamically changing workloads and priorities. One of the key requirements for the System/38 instruction interface was to provide efficient support in this type of environment for application requirements such as multiprogramming and data base operations. This centralization of function in the machine simplifies the user programming task and reduces overhead in a dynamic multi-user environment.

Two examples of this system function support will be described here — multiprogramming and data base. Similar high levels of machine capability exist in other major functional areas such as I/O.

System/38 supports multiprogramming through the concept of processes. A process is similar to a task in other systems and is the basis for managing work in the machine. The user of the System/38 instruction interface controls the number of processes currently initiated, the priority of each process, and the relationship of one process to another, that is, with respect to processor utilization and storage utilization. The machine then allocates the processor and storage resources based on these parameters as well as on the current status of the process, for example, waiting or dispatchable.

This level of multiprogramming support in the System/38 machine offers advantages like these:

- A single resource management mechanism is applied to processing across all system activities. This reduces overhead and results in better management of resources in a complex and dynamic environment.

- Other efficient resource management mechanisms can be used to take advantage of hardware characteristics without programming dependencies.

Similarly, the System/38 machine provides the basic functional building blocks for a high-function integrated data base. Data base objects include a comprehensive set of functions supporting different access mechanisms, file sharing, record format definition and mapping, efficient record retrieval, update, add, and delete. This allows, for example, a data base file structure to be defined that maps a single physical file into records with multiple formats and content. In addition, a single physical data base file may have multiple indexes (access paths) defined over it, all of which are concurrently updated when the file is changed. Each user of the file may view the data in the form suitable to a particular application.

Overhead Considerations

One of the major problems inherent in the implementation of a high-level instruction interface such as that provided for the System/38 is overhead. In order to reduce the potential overhead, and also to facilitate future extensions, the System/38 instruction interface definition does not require a directly executable implementation of the instruction interface. The instructions and the operand definition dictionary are presented to the instruction interface and are translated into an executable microcode structure called a program object. The internal microcode format is not apparent at the interface. Figure 4, System/38 Executable Program Creation, illustrates this process.

Having an executable program creation step allows the system to have the advantage of both a high-level instruction interface and reduced overhead at execution time.

In addition, direct support of high-use functions in the System/38 instruction interface, as previously described, is itself an approach toward reducing *system* overhead. A single implementation of a complex function that can be applied system-wide reduces overhead.

Also, by implementing these functions in the machine, hardware facilities can reduce the overhead that is associated with the higher level implementation typically required in programming.

FIGURE 4
System/38 Executable Program Creation

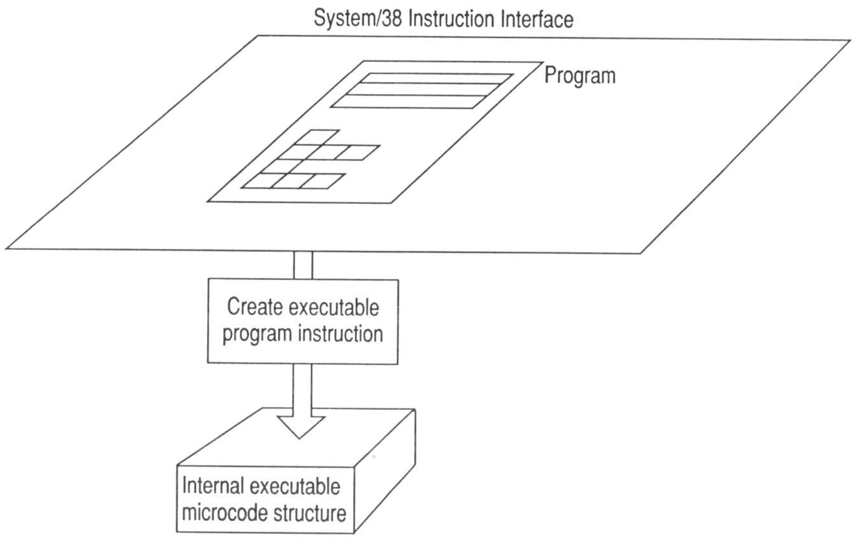

Summary

The IBM System/38 provides a new type of machine instruction interface that comprises a high level of function together with structures similar to high-level language structures and includes computation, addressing, and such traditional programming functions as process (task) management, resource management, and device handling. This new machine was designed to satisfy major design objectives for the entire system — hardware, microprogramming, and program products. The concept of a high-level machine has been discussed in the literature and has been experimented with in both industrial and research environments; however, System/38 is the first IBM system to bring the advantages of a high-level machine to the business user.

System/38 Object-Oriented Architecture

States that the construct, "object," is of central significance in System/38. Discusses the concepts, purpose, and characteristics of System/38 machine objects

by K.W. Pinnow, J.G. Ranweiler, and J.F. Miller

System/38 provides a range of capability not previously available in low-cost data processing systems. This capability is made possible by the use of a number of technical innovations. One of these is the *object.* This article discusses objects — the means through which information is stored and processed on System/38. Included are the concepts, purpose, and characteristics of System/38 machine objects and their use by the Control Program Facility (CPF).

Object Concepts

Previous machine instruction sets have provided bit- and byte-string manipulation capabilities. The machine instruction set in System/38 provides similar functions and also provides machine instructions that operate on complex data structures to accomplish high-level functions.

Some of the data structures are similar to such things as programs and data files in conventional systems. Some are unique to System/38. The data structures that appear in the instruction interface are collectively categorized as objects.

An object is brought into existence through execution of a create instruction. The user controls the creation of the object through a template [Alls78] that provides a set of attributes and values that are to apply to the new object. The new object also has operational characteristics that define the set of functions that may be accomplished through it. Examples of object attributes and operations are shown in Figure 1.

The three examples of attributes illustrated in Figure 1 are (1) a *name* that permits symbolic reference to the object, (2) an *existence* that specifies whether implicit destruction is allowed, and (3) *ownership* that identifies who, if anyone, owns the object.

The set of instructions that are operationally meaningful to an object consist of *generic* operations that apply to all types of objects and *unique* operations that apply to a specific type object. The generic operations are primarily *authorization*, *addressing*-, and *resource*-related [BTR78]. The unique operations include a *destroy* that removes the object from the system, some form of *materialize* that identifies the objects attributes or content, and sometimes a *modify* that changes the attributes of the object. Many other unique operations exist that are not identified in Figure 1.

FIGURE 1

Some Examples of Object Attributes and Operations in System/38

Object	Attributes	Name	
		Ownership	
		Existence	
	Generic operations	Explicit functions	Authorization
			Addressing
			Resource
		Implicit functions	Atomicity
			Lock enforcement
			Authorization enforcement
	Unique operations	Explicit functions	Materialization
			Modification
			Destruction
		Implicit functions	Atomicity
			Lock enforcement
			Authorization enforcement

Each operation, whether generic or unique, also provides significant implicit functions. The implicit functions are *authorization, lock enforcement,* and *atomic* (exclusive) *operation.*

Object Purpose

The concept of an object gives a common attribute to a group of data structures and enables the definition of an interface that produces a number of benefits.

The existence of objects allows systematic manipulation of structures. Their presence permits the definition of an instruction interface that is consistent across a wide range of supervisor and computational instructions.

Objects exist to make users independent of specific implementation techniques used in the machine. Since it is necessary that users control the data used in supervisor functions, object management capability is provided. When a request for a high-level machine function is made, a specific instruction operator (operation code), optionally an attribute template, and an object are specified. System/38 uses the object to accumulate results of operations, to store them in such a way that they are safe from inadvertent modification, and to assure that they are available for subsequent operations.

Objects exist to make the user independent of the addressing structure actually used in the hardware. Although main storage and auxiliary storage exist in System/38, users are shielded from the mechanics of actually addressing that storage. In other words, objects remove the traditional responsibility of mapping data onto physical storage.

Object Characteristics

For an object like a program, creation establishes the essential content of the object, and subsequent instructions use it operationally. For other objects, the creation is primarily a space allocation mechanism for which succeeding operations establish the content. For example, once a data space has been created, records may be inserted into it. Management of the size of an object and changes to that size are generally transparent to the System/38 users.

All System/38 machine objects are *encapsulated.* Encapsulation is the process of accepting a definition of an object through a create instruction and using this definition to produce an object whose internal structure is only accessible to the machine. Objects are encapsulated to maintain the integrity of the internal structure and to permit different implementations of the machine instruction interface without impact to its users.

It is possible to associate an unencapsulated (byte string) area with each object. This byte-string area is referred to as a space and is up to 16 megabytes of virtual storage into which the machine user can build control blocks of other control information or data. As a degenerate case of an object, one with essentially no encapsulated portion, a space exists as an independent object. Whether it is an object itself or is associated with another object, a space has its size modified through explicit instructions by the machine user.

System/38 Machine Objects

The following lists and briefly describes the objects of the System/38 machine instruction set:

Access group. An object that permits the physical grouping of other objects to achieve more efficient movement of the objects between main storage and auxiliary storage.

Context. An object that contains the *type*, *subtype*, and *name* of other objects to allow addressability.

Controller description. An object that represents an I/O controller for a cluster of I/O devices or a station that attaches groups of communication devices over the same data communication link.

Cursor. An object used to provide addressability into a data space.

Data space. An object used to store data base records of one format.

Data space index. An object used to provide a logical ordering of records stored in a data space.

Index. An object used to store and automatically order data.

Logical unit description. An object that represents a physical I/O device.

Network description. An object that represents a network port of the system.

Process control space. An object used to contain process execution.

Program. An object for uniquely selecting and ordering machine interface instructions.

Queue. An object used to communicate between processes, and between a process and a device.

Space. An object used for storing pointers and scalars.

User profile. An object used to identify a valid user of the machine interface.

CPF Use of Machine Objects

The CPF extends the object-oriented approach of the machine and provides its users with a high-level, object-oriented interface [Harv78]. All data stored on the system by CPF users is stored in object form and is processable in terms of control language commands and high-level languages. To the user of CPF, objects are named collections of data, and the functions associated with objects provide the vehicle for processing this data and obtaining work from the system. The 19 objects presented to the user at the CPF interface include conventional constructs, such as files and programs, as well as constructs that are unique to System/38, such as job descriptions and message queues [Deme78].

The functions that CPF provides for its objects include some that are object-type-specific and some that are generic with respect to object type. The object-type-specific functions define and limit the way in which an object can be used while the generic functions provide for authorization, locking, saving, restoring, dumping, moving, and renaming objects. Through the generic functions, the user has a way of managing objects once they exist.

Objects are brought into existence through the specification of a create command that defines the name, attributes, and initial value of the object to be created. Each object is assigned a type and subtype as a part of the creation process. The object's type is determined by the kind of machine object created to support the object that the CPF user wishes to create; the object's subtype designates the use that CPF intends for the machine object. Each unique use that the CPF makes of a machine object is assigned a unique subtype identifier. This aspect of the design is important because it is through the use of unique types and subtypes that the system can ensure that each type of object is always used in the way it was intended. After an object has been created, it remains on the system until it is explicitly deleted via a delete command. At the time an object is created, CPF places the name of the object into a machine object known as a *context.*

Contexts are presented to the user as libraries. Because the functions associated with contexts are capable of finding an object based on its name, type, and sub-type, libraries can be considered as a catalog or container for the user-created objects. Whenever an object is to be found, CPF initiates a search for the object either in a single library or through an ordered list of libraries that the CPF maintains with each executing job. When the list of libraries is used to find an object, each successive library in the list is searched until the object is found. Using the list of libraries to find the objects to be processed is advantageous because the same commands or program can perform functions on different objects merely by changing the order of the libraries in the library list.

CPF maintains descriptive information for all objects and provides functions for the retrieval and display of this data. The descriptive information records who the object owner is, when the object was created, where the object has most recently been saved, and text information provided by the user to further describe the object.

An important feature of CPF object architecture is the manner in which CPF objects are constructed. CPF uses machine objects as building blocks to produce the objects that CPF users see. Figure 2 shows an example of how one kind of Control Program Facility object is constructed.

In this example, four types of machine objects (a data space, a data space index, a cursor, and a space) are combined to produce the higher level CPF object known to the user as a *data base file*. CPF manages the individual pieces of a file in a way that allows the user to perceive the file as a single entity. For example, the separate pieces of the file come into existence when a single create-file command is processed and remain in existence until the file is explicitly deleted. Thus, the user is relieved of the complexity and organizational details of the data and can process it as a logical entity. When lower level objects are put together to form a higher level object, the higher level object is known as a composite object. CPF object architecture permits any type of System/38 machine or CPF object to be combined to produce a new type of object. In fact, CPF-provided functions for managing objects are table-driven, based on unique object type and subtype combinations. This aspect of the design means that the object-oriented approach can be quickly and easily extended. It also permits new kinds of objects to be compatibly introduced later on in the life of the system.

The key advantage of the System/38 building block architecture, however, is that the implicit functions provided by the machine for its objects are made directly available to the end user in a consistent manner. For example, implicit in all CPF objects are the machine-provided functions of security, lock enforcement, and object resolution by name. The benefits of this architecture are readily apparent when one contrasts the approach of System/38 with that of other systems having different addressing structures for different collections of data, added-on security functions, and user interfaces that require knowledge of the physical aspects of data organization.

Summary

The object orientation of the System/38 machine and CPF interfaces permits common provision of function at each interface. With machine-inter-

FIGURE 2
An Example of How One Kind of Control Program Facility Object is Constructed

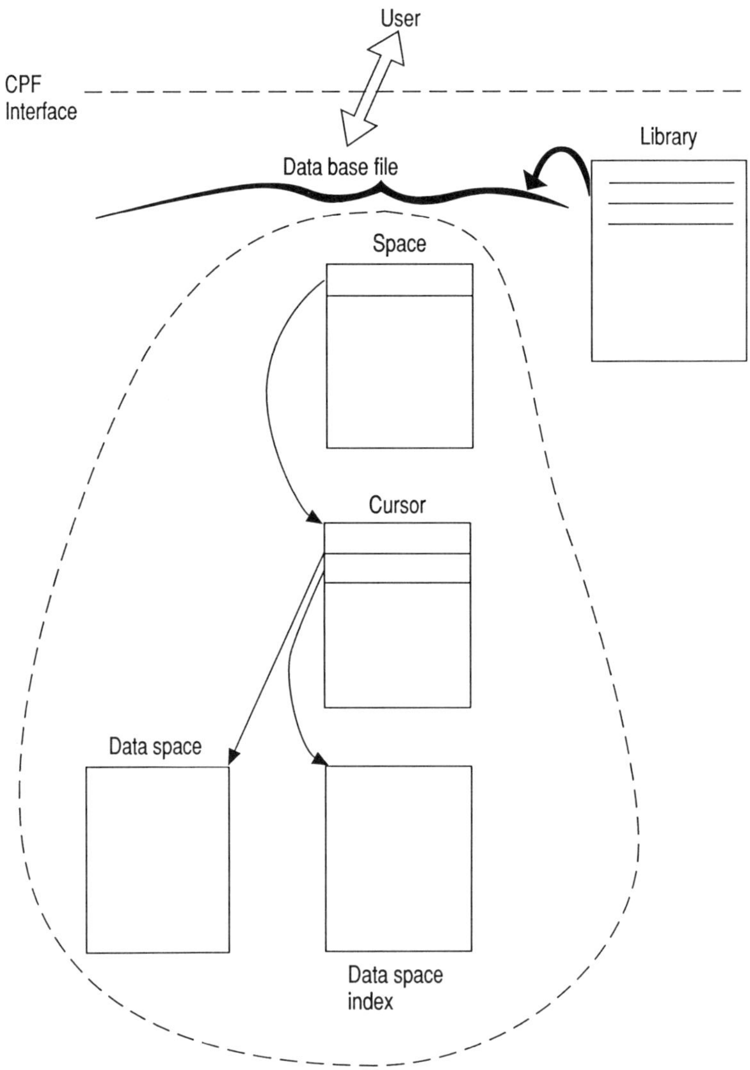

face objects, the hardware addressing mechanism and the internal format and organization of data are transparent to the user; serialization and authorization functions are implicit in the objects. The key characteristic that makes this possible is encapsulation of objects in the machine-instruction interface. Since CPF uses the objects of the System/38 instruction interface as building blocks, its objects possess all the function of the machine objects.

System/38 Addressing and Authorization

Discusses addressing, authorization, locking, and synchronization in System/38

by V. Berstis, C.D. Truxal, and J.G. Ranweiler

The high-level machine interface of System/38 achieves user independence from the internal machine implementation primarily through the use of an object-oriented architecture. Objects representing storage for constructs such as programs, processes, and data base files are accessed through a consistent, integrated addressing structure. Because authority enforcement and control of shared objects are critical in multiprogramming environments, these functions have been incorporated into the addressing path. This article describes some of the key features of the addressing design of System/38 and how they are presented to the user through the Control Program Facility (CPF), which is described by Harvey and Conway [Harv78].

Objects and Spaces

Before addressing can be described, it is necessary to define what is accessed. Everything stored in the system is an *object* (see Figure 1), which consists of a functional portion and an associated space (see Pinnow, et al [PRM78]). The functional part of an object is used to implement a particular construct. For example, the functional part of a program object is created by the translation of System/38 machine instructions into microcode. The program is said to be *encapsulated* because there is no direct access to the storage used to support it. Instead, the object is manipulated at a high level through the System/38 instruction set. In this way, encapsulation ensures the functional integrity of all objects.

The *associated space* portion of an object is a region of bytes that can be directly manipulated by the machine user. The space is associated with the functional part of the object and provides a convenient way of storing additional (user-defined) data pertinent to that objects usage. One type of object, called a *space object*, has no functional part. Its associated space is used to provide storage for control blocks, buffers, pointers, and other data.

FIGURE 1
System/38 Objects and Pointers

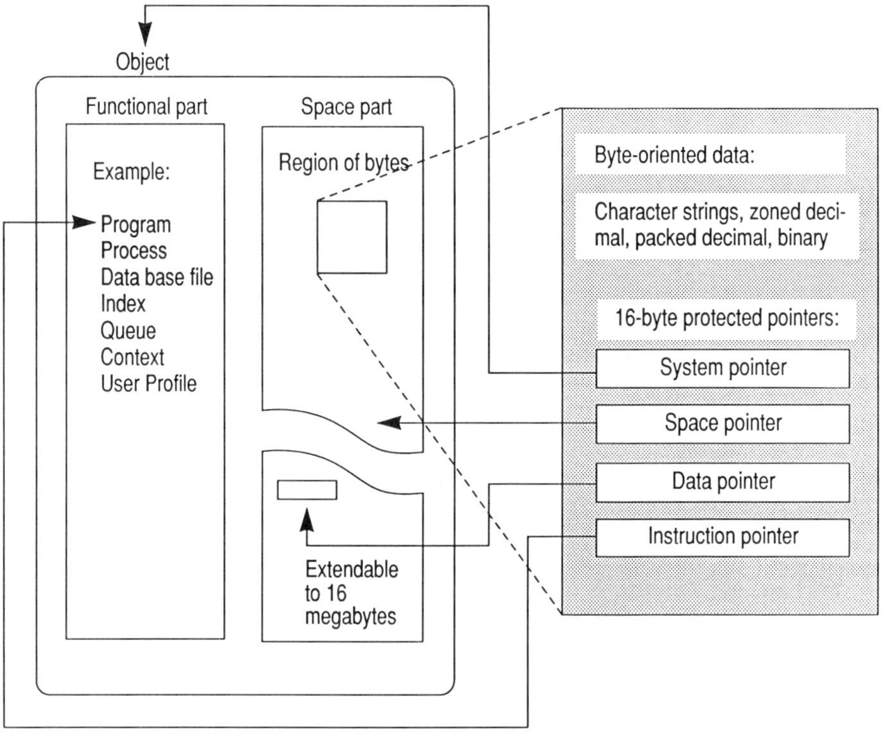

Pointers

There are four different types of pointers. *System pointers* address objects; *space pointers* and *data pointers* address specific byte locations within the space portion of an object; and *instructional pointers* control execution flow. This article covers object addressing through system pointers.

A *system pointer*, used to address an object, contains both the location of the object in storage and object usage rights, as will be discussed later. Only specific System/38 instructions can create pointers. Although pointers can be copied, the user cannot construct pointers by bit manipulation. As a result of these properties, System/38 has the basic elements of *capability based addressing* [Lind76].

Name Resolution

A system pointer exists in one of two states: resolved or unresolved. In the *unresolved state*, the pointer specifies the name of an object and not its location. When the pointer is first referenced (see Figure 2), the machine

FIGURE 2
The Object Access Path

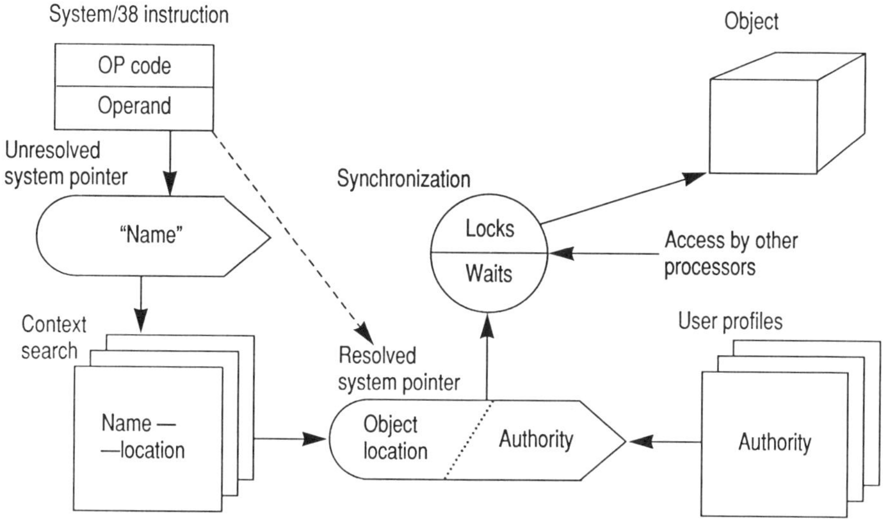

searches for an object having the specified name. Once found, the resulting object location is stored in the pointer, thereby eliminating subsequent searches. The pointer is then said to be in the *resolved state*.

The search performed during pointer resolution involves the use of objects called *contexts*, containing object names and locations. Various execution environments are obtained by specifying an ordered list of contexts to be searched. For example, the production and test versions of files can be located through different contexts. Therefore, by simply exchanging the contexts searched, either programming environment can be achieved.

Authorization

The ability to control pointer resolution in the machine is not sufficient to effectively control the users access to objects because it is an all or nothing type of control. The System/38 object authorization mechanism provides the fineness (granularity) of control needed for the wide range of operations performed on objects.

Every reference to an object requires that the user have the appropriate authority for the operation to be performed; otherwise, the operation is suppressed and the attempted violation is recorded. The authority checking function is uniformly applied to all types of objects. Separate authorities (retrieve or update, for example) can be granted to individual users or to all users (the public). Therefore, a user's authority can be limited to what is exactly necessary for an application. For example, a user might be authorized to retrieve data from a data base file but not to update or destroy the file.

Sources of Authority

A prerequisite for authority verification is the identification of the user. This prerequisite is satisfied through the use of an object called the *user profile*, which identifies the user and the user's authority. Every process is initiated with a specified user profile as the primary source of authority. Object authorities can be granted to or revoked from a user profile, thus providing control over the authority available to the process. Objects can also be publicly authorized, thereby eliminating the need to explicitly authorize every user profile.

In some applications, subprograms require a different amount of authority than that available to the calling program. To accomplish this, programs can *adopt* a user profile (Figure 3). The adopted user profile adds its authority to what is already present in a process. When the program calls other programs, the adopted user profile authorities can be optionally propagated to the called program. This provides considerable flexibility in controlling the security environment.

Once authority to an object has been established, it can be optionally stored in the pointer to that object. This provides faster authority verification than with unauthorized pointers.

Other Authorizations

One type of authority not related to objects is the *privileged instruction authority.* Such authorization is used for process initiation, user profile creation, machine reconfiguration, etc. Other *special authorities* range over many machine functions rather than specific instructions. For example, *all-object* special authority permits unlimited use of all objects in the system. The control of storage resources is another wide-range authority. The storage occupied by objects is charged against the *storage limit* of the user profile (the owner) under which they were created. Owners have implied object authority to the objects they own.

Locking and Synchronization

The authority mechanism of System/38 ensures that an application accesses only objects within its intended rights. When multiple applications attempt to reference the same objects concurrently, additional controls are provided to prevent interface. System/38 incorporates implicit synchronization functions into the object access implementation to accomplish this. For

FIGURE 3
User Profiles as Sources of Authority

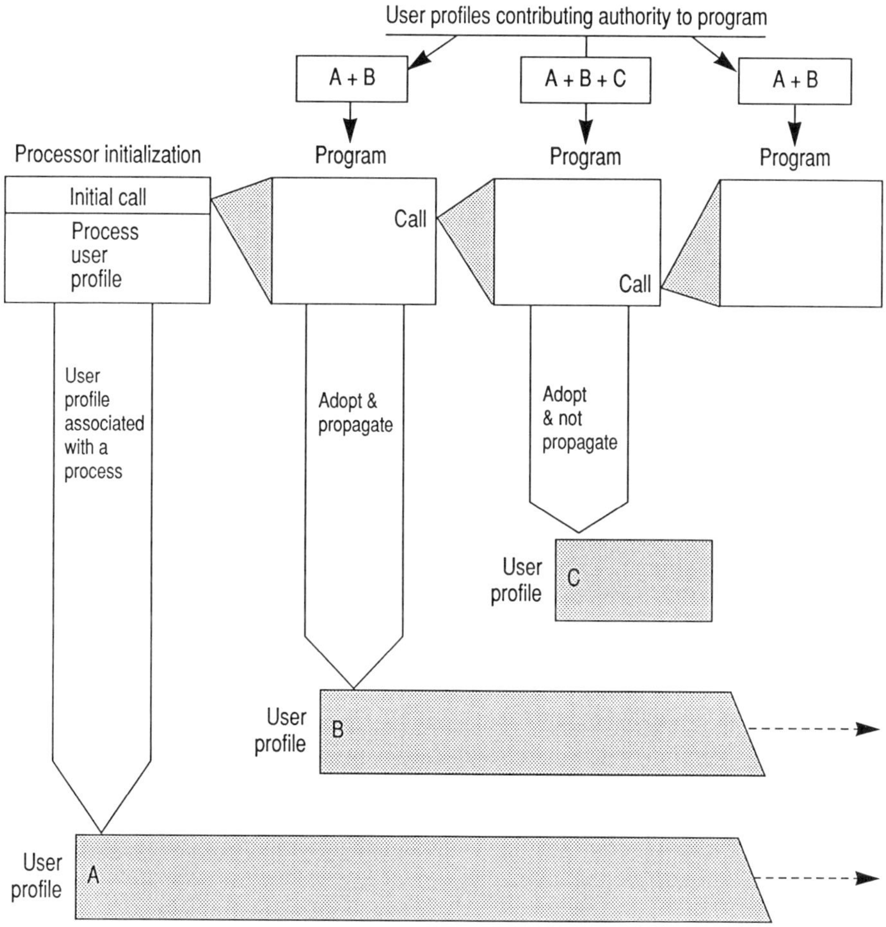

example, if one process is updating an object while another process is attempting to access the same object, the operations are automatically serialized. On the other hand, if both processes are retrieving data from the same object, the operations are allowed to proceed simultaneously. Therefore, contention is reduced and integrity of the object is ensured.

Explicit synchronization is available to the user in the form of *locks*. By locking an object, the user can control the access of other users to the object. Entire sequences of operations can be serialized when required to maintain data integrity. In addition, second level locks in data base files reduce much of the contention that would be present if the entire file were locked.

Synchronization functions complete the machine addressing path, which starts with the object name and continues through pointer resolution and authority verification.

Addressing Path Usage

The Control Program Facility (CPF) is an IBM program product providing the user a high-function, ease-of-use interface to the machine [Harv78]. With the high-level machine facilities available in the System/38, the CPF addressing and authorization function uses both capability-based and symbolic object addressing with authority validation at execution time.

CPF uses machine pointer resolution, authorization management, and locking to implement internal CPF security and synchronization. It provides these facilities to the user through CPF interfaces.

Within CPF, the work management component isolates and protects its critical resource control and scheduling functions by executing them under the system user profile. The remaining CPF modules execute under the user's profile. Thus, the machine authorization management directly validates the user's authority to perform every requested function on any specified object. Everything in CPF is an object. I/O devices and Control Language commands are objects, as are more typically files, programs, and libraries. Because of this, an installation can control system resources to the extent desired.

Installation Authorization

This control of an installation's resources has led to the concept of one specific user as an installation's *security administrator*. This user is entrusted with authorities allowing system-wide control of all users and their resources. A set of IBM-supplied user profiles is delivered with CPF, including one for the security officer. This profile has all-object authority, as well as authority to create and modify user profiles. Therefore, the security officer can enroll users on the system and control their use of system resources. When a user profile is created or modified, special authorities, resource allocation parameters, and a user password can be specified. The user password is for verification of user identity at sign-on and for determining the user profile associated with a process.

Once the user is executing, functions are performed by executing programs or commands. These functions reference objects (such as files) by name, and CPF locates the object through the use of the machine-addressing facilities. This is easily implemented because contexts (objects that contain names of other objects [PRM78]) are used by CPF as system and user libraries. When an object such as a program or file is created, it is placed in a library. Subsequent referencing of the object initiates pointer resolution, and the machine not only locates the object, but validates the current user's authority to the object and determines whether serialization of an operation is necessary. To expedite authority checking, CPF requests that the authority be set in the pointer for future use.

CPF Object Authorities

When a user creates an object, it can be declared public or private. Subsequently, any of the objects authorities can be granted or revoked to individual users or the public. Display commands are also available to report object authority.

Summary

The System/38 is based on an object-oriented architecture in which everything in the system is an object. An object can be referenced by its name, which is used in a pointer resolution process that includes authorization and synchronization functions. The resulting resolved pointer can contain object location and authority to avoid subsequent searches. The machine enforces authority requirements on every object referenced, verifying the authority from the pointer or user profile(s). The user profile is an object that identifies a user in the system and contains all of that user's authorities. The CPF uses the machine addressing, authorization, and synchronization facilities, and provides their function to the user.

The System/38 thus delivers the flexibility of named object addressing and the integrity of machine-enforced authorization and synchronization of those objects.

Appendix A — References

[Alls78] Allsen, J.K., "System/38 Common Code Generation," page 100, *IBM System/38 Technical Developments.* White Plains, NY: IBM, 1978. G580-0237.

[BTR78] Berstis, V.; Truxal, C.D.; and Ranweiler, J.G.; "System/38 Addressing and Authorization," page 51, *IBM System/38 Technical Developments.* White Plains, NY: IBM, 1978. G580-0237. (Reprinted in Appendix A of this book.)

[Deme78] Demers, R.A., "The Generalized Message Handler in System/38," page 97, *IBM System/38 Technical Developments.* White Plains, NY: IBM, 1978. G580-0237.

[FCL78] French, R.E.; Collins, R.W.; and Loen, L.W.; "System/38 Machine Storage Management," page 63, *IBM System/38 Technical Developments.* White Plains, NY: IBM, 1978. G580-0237.

[Harv78] Harvey, D.G., "Introduction to the System/38 Control Program Facility," page 74, *IBM System/38 Technical Developments.* White Plains, NY: IBM, 1978. G580-0237.

[HB78] Howard, P.H., and Borgendale, K.W., "System/38 Machine Indexing Support," page 67, *IBM System/38 Technical Developments.* White Plains, NY: IBM, 1978. G580-0237.

[Henr78] Henry, G.G., "Introduction to IBM System/38 Architecture," page 3, *IBM System/38 Technical Developments.* White Plains, NY: IBM, 1978. G580-0237.

[HS78] Hoffman, R.L., and Soltis, F.G., "Hardware Organization of the System/38," page 19, *IBM System/38 Technical Developments.* White Plains, NY: IBM, 1978. G580-0237.

[Lind76] Linden, Theodore A., "Operating System Structures to Support Security and Reliable Software," *Computing Surveys,* Vol. 8, No. 4, 409 (1976).

[PRM78] Pinnow, K.W.; Ranweiler, J.G.; and Miller, J.F.; "System/38 Object-Oriented Architecture," page 55, *IBM System/38 Technical Developments.* White Plains, NY: IBM, 1978. G580-0237. (Reprinted in Appendix A of this book.)

[WA78] Watson, C.T., and Aberle, G.F., "System/38 Machine Data Base Support," page 59, *IBM System/38 Technical Developments.* White Plains, NY: IBM, 1978. G580-0237.

References

[ACM91] Combined market research study of the *Communications of the ACM* readership conducted by the Gallup Organization of Princeton, New Jersey in 1991 and the Harvey Research Organization of Fairport, New York in 1992.

[Berg91] Bergland, G.D. "A Guided Tour of Program Design Methodologies," *IEEE Computer*, October 1981.

[Booc83] Booch, G. *Software Engineering with Ada.* Reading, Mass: Addison-Wesley, 1983.

[Booc91] Booch, G. *Object-Oriented Design with Applications.* Redwood City, CA: Benjamin/Cummings, 1991.

[Broo87] Brooks, F.P. "No Silver Bullet: Essence and Accidents of Software Engineering," *IEEE Computer*, April 1987.

[Cox84] Cox, B. "Message/Object Programming: An Evolutionary Change in Programming Technology," *IEEE Software*, January 1984. Reprinted in *Object-Oriented Computing Concepts* [Pete90].

[CN91] Cox, B., and Novobilski, J. *Object-Oriented Programming: An Evolutionary Approach* 2nd ed. Reading, Mass: Addison-Wesley, 1991.

[DDH72] Dahl, O-J.; Dijkstra, E.W.; and Hoare, C.A. *Structured Programming.* London, England: Academic Press, 1972.

[DS90] DeGrace, P., and Stahl, L.H. *Wicked Problems, Righteous Solutions: A Catalogue of Modern Software Engineering Paradigms.* Englewood Cliffs, NJ: Prentice-Hall, 1990.

[Dijk72] Dijkstra, E.W. "The Humble Programmer," *Communications of the ACM*, October 1972. Reprinted in *Classics in Software Engineering* [Your79].

[Hoar72] Hoare, C.A. "Notes on Data Structuring," *Structured Programming*. London, England: Academic Press, 1972.

[King89] King, R. "My Cat Is Object-Oriented," *Object-Oriented Concepts, Databases, and Applications*. ed. W. Kim and F. H. Lochovsky. Reading, MA: Addison-Wesley, 1989.

[Koen93] Koenig, A. "What do you do after you say 'Hello World'?", *Journal of Object-Oriented Programming*, September 1993.

[LZ80] Liskov, B., and Zilles, S. "Programming with Abstract Data Types," *SIGPLAN Notices*, April 1974. Reprinted in *Programming Language Design*. ed. A. Wasserman. New York, NY: Computer Society Press of the IEEE, 1980.

[LG86] Liskov, B., and Guttag, J. *Abstraction and Specification in Program Development*. Cambridge, Mass: MIT Press, 1986.

[Meye88] Meyer, B. *Object-Oriented Software Construction*. Englewood Cliffs, NJ: Prentice Hall, 1988.

[Nels91] Nelson, M.L. "An Object-Oriented Tower of Babel," *OOPS Messenger*, July 1991.

[ND81] Nygaard, K.; and Dahl, O-J. "The Development of the Simula Languages," *History of Programming Languages*. ed. R. Wexelblat. New York, NY: Academic Press, 1981.

[OT93] Ong, C.L., and Tsai, W.T. "Class and Object Extraction from Imperative Code," *Journal of Object-Oriented Programming*, March/April 1993.

[Parn72a] Parnas, D. "A Technique for Software Module Specification with Examples," *Communications of the ACM*, May 1972. Reprinted in *Writings of the Revolution* [Your82].

[Parn72b] Parnas, D. "On the Criteria to be Used in Decomposing Systems into Modules," *Communications of the ACM*, December 1972. Reprinted in *Classics in Software Engineering* [Your79].

[PCW85] Parnas, D.; Clements, P.; and Weiss, D. "The Modular Structure of Complex Systems," *IEEE Transactions on Software*

Engineering, March 1985. Reprinted in *Object-Oriented Computing Implementations* [Pete87].

[Pete87] Peterson, G.E. ed. *Object-Oriented Computing Implementations.* New York, NY: Computer Society Press of the IEEE.

[Pete90] Peterson, G.E. ed. *Object-Oriented Computing Concepts.* New York, NY: Computer Society Press of the IEEE.

[Rent82] Rentsch, T. "Object-Oriented Programming," *SIGPLAN Notices*, September 1982. Reprinted in *Object-Oriented Computing Concepts* [Pete90].

[Robs81] Robson, D. "Object-Oriented Software Systems," *BYTE*, August 1981. Reprinted in *Object-Oriented Computing Concepts* [Pete90].

[Saun89] Saunders, J.H. "A Survey of Object-Oriented Programming Languages," *Journal of Object-Oriented Programming*, March/April 1989.

[Sess92] Sessions, R. *Class Construction in C and C++.* Englewood Cliffs, NJ: Prentice Hall, 1992.

[Shaw84] Shaw, M. "Abstraction Techniques in Modern Programming Languages," *IEEE Software*, October 1984. Reprinted in *Object-Oriented Computing Implementations* [Pete87].

[Snyd86] Snyder, A. "Encapsulation and Inheritance in Object-Oriented Programming Languages," *OOPSLA 1986 Proceedings.* New York, NY: ACM, 1986.

[Snyd93] Snyder, A. "The Essence of Objects: Concepts and Terms," *IEEE Software*, January 1993.

[SB86] Stefik, M., and Bobrow, D. "Object-Oriented Programming: Themes and Variations," *AI Magazine*, Winter 1986. Reprinted in *Object-Oriented Computing Concepts* [Pete90].

[Stro88] Stroustrup, B. "What is Object-Oriented Programming?" *IEEE Software*, May 1988.

[Stro91] Stroustrup, B. *The C++ Programming Language* 2nd ed. Reading, MA: Addison-Wesley, 1991.

[Tayl90] Taylor, D. *Object-Oriented Technology: A Manager's Guide.* Almeda, CA: Servio, 1990.

[Wegn76] Wegner, P. "Programming Languages — the First 25 Years," *IEEE Transactions on Computers*, December 1976. Reprinted in *Programming Languages: A Grand Tour* 3rd ed., ed. E. Horowitz. Rockville, MD: Computer Science Press, 1987.

[Wegn87] Wegner, P. "Dimensions of Object-Based Language Design," *OOPSLA 1987 Proceedings.* New York, NY: ACM, 1987.

[Wegn92] Wegner, P. "Dimensions of Object-Oriented Modelling," *IEEE Computer*, October 1992.

[WP88] Wiener, R.S., and Pinson, L.J. *An Introduction to Object-Oriented Programming and C++.* Reading, Mass: Addison-Wesley, 1988.

[Wirt85] Wirth, N. *Programming in Modula-2.* Berlin, Germany: Springer-Verlag, 1985.

[Your79] Yourdon, E.N. ed. *Classics in Software Engineering.* New York, NY: Yourdon Press, 1979.

[Your82] Yourdon, E.N. ed. *Writings of the Revolution.* New York, NY: Yourdon Press, 1982.

Glossary

abstract class — a *class* for which no *instances* are created

abstract data type — combines concepts of *encapsulation* and *procedural abstraction* to define a set of data items and its associated operations

abstraction — simplified description of a system that excludes unnecessary details

class — a template that describes one or more similar *objects*. In object-oriented programming languages, it is a *user-defined data type*

data abstraction — *See abstract data type*

dynamic binding — associating a *message* to the corresponding *method* code at runtime

encapsulation — to prevent access to a given entity except through defined interfaces

information hiding — *See encapsulation*

inheritance — a code-sharing mechanism that allows expression of the difference between an existing *class* and a new class

instance — a physical *object* associated with a given *class*

message — the means of invoking an object's *method*, the act of which is called *sending a message* to the object

method — an operation defined upon an *object*

object — data that is *encapsulated* by associated *abstract* operations

object-based	a system that supports and enforces the concept of *objects*
object-oriented	a system that supports and enforces the concepts of *objects*, *classes*, and *inheritance*
overloading	using the same name or operator to represent different operations
polymorphism	combination of *overloading* and *dynamic binding* so that the same message sent to different objects invokes the appropriate method for the target object
procedural abstraction	an *abstraction* of a sequence of operations into a single operation, such as a subroutine
static binding	associating a *message* to the corresponding *method* code at program-creation time
subclass	a *class* that *inherits* from one or more classes
superclass	a *class* that is *inherited* from another class
user-defined data type	a user-defined abstract data type that the compiler treats in the same way as the language's built-in data types

Index

A

Abstract class, 36-37
Abstract data type, 10-12
  defined, 10
  RPG/400 file type and, 10
  as user-defined data type, 10
Abstraction, 9-12
  data, 10-12
  defined, 2, 9
  procedural, 9
  using, 9
Access-specifier, 53
  private, 53, 56, 65
  protected, 53, 65, 67
    using, 68
  public, 53, 65
  See also Class member
Ada, 3, 15, 35
  package construct, 10
  package example, 10-12
    illustrated, 11

B

BASE class, 34, 35-36
  inheriting from, 37
Binding, 40-42
  to class code, 41
  dynamic, 41
  carly, 41
  late, 41
  static, 41
  See also Polymorphism

C

C++, 3, 35, 50-52
  constructors, 58, 60
  `crtdtaara` function, 54
  design goals, 51
  destructors, 58-60
  exception handling, 75
  `friend` specifier, 71-72
  history of, 51
  learning, 75
  main function, 55, 64, 67, 74
  multiple inheritance, 67-69
    defining derived class
    with, 68
    illustrated example, 69
  operator overloading, 60-64
  overloading and, 39
  polymorphism and, 42
  `rtvdtaara` function, 54
  stream class library, 74
  stream class operator, 56, 74
  stream manipulator, 56
  templates, 74-75
  virtual functions, 72-74
  See also C++ class
C++ class, 30, 53-56
  access-specifiers, 53
  definitions, 53
    example, 54
  derived, 65-69
    defining with multiple
    inheritance, 68
    illustrated example, 66
    syntax for defining, 65
  using, 57-64
  See also C++
CHGDTAATA operation, 17, 19
  with OOP object, 20
Class, 15, 29-32

abstract, 36-37
advantages of, 31-32
date, 31
defined, 26, 29
definitions in OOPLs, 30
illustrated, 29
instances and, 29, 30-32, 35
objects and, 31
OS/400 object model and, 29-30
subclass, 33
superclass, 33
See also C++ class; Inheritance
Class library, 32
Class member, 53
DTAARA, 53-54
function invocation, 55
protected, 67
See also Access-specifier; Member function
Constructor, 58-60
defining, 58
using class with, 59
See also Destructor
Coupling, 6

D

Date class, 60-64
member functions, 60-61
partial definition for, 61
Date variables, 24
encapsulating, 25
incorrect access of, 24
objects for each, 25
OOP model and, 24-25
Derived class, 65-69
defining with multiple inheritance, 68
illustrated example, 66
syntax for defining, 65
Destructor, 58-60
defining, 58
using class with, 59
See also Constructor
DSPF class, 34
DSPFD in, 36
inheritance, 35
DTAARA class, 29-30
`base_class` and, 65-67
defining constructor/destructor for, 58
member functions, 53-54
definitions, 59
using, 55
DTAARA object, 17
methods, 17-18
underlying structure of, 29
Dynamic binding, 41

E

Encapsulation, 5-8

F

FAXF object, 43
FILE class, 34, 35-36
methods, 35
`friend` specifier, 71-72
using, 72
Functional decomposition, 6-7

G

General object model, 13-15
See also Object model

I

Information hiding. *See* Encapsulation
Inheritance, 15, 33-37, 67
advantages of, 37
defined, 26-27, 33
illustrated, 33
methods and, 35-36
multiple, 34, 67-69

See also Class; Derived class
Instance, 29
classes and, 30-32, 35

M

Member function, 53-56, 74
invoking, 57
See also Class member
Message/object model, 21
language implementation, 27
operator/operand model vs., 21
See also Object model
Method, 17
excluding, 36
inheritance and, 35-36
superclass, redefining, 36
Modula-2, 3, 15, 35
Modula-2 module, 7-8
definition part, 7
implementation part, 7
partial definition of, 8
Multiple inheritance, 34
C++, 67-69
defining derived class with, 68
illustrated example, 69
See also Inheritance

O

Object-based system, 35
Object model, 13-18
comparison of, 45-47
general, 13-15
OOP, 17-18, 24-25, 45-47
OS/400, 16-17, 29-30, 35, 45-47
Object-oriented design, 7
Object-oriented programming languages. *See* OOPL
Object-oriented system, 35
Object, 15
class and, 31
in OOPLs, 23
OS/400, 16-17, 19
components of, 21
passive entity, 46
programming with, 22-26
of same class, 26
Simula, 49
using, 19-28
OOPL, 49-52
class code invocation in, 30
class definition in, 30
objects in, 23
polymorphism in, 42
See also C++; Simula; Smalltalk
Operator/operand model, 19, 46
message/object model vs., 21
OS/400, 21-22
See also Object model
Operator overloading, 60-64
code readability and, 61
illustrated example, 62
using, 63
See also Overloading
OS/400
architecture, 47
implementation, 46-47
object model, 2, 16-17
classes and, 29-30
illustrated, 16, 45
OOP comparison, 45-47
object, 16-17
components, 21
as passive entity, 46
using, 19
operand/operator model, 21-22
Overloading, 39-40
advantages, 39, 40
defined, 39

function and procedure names, 40
name, 40
operator, 60-64
See also Binding; Polymorphism

P

Polymorphism, 42-43
advantages, 42-43
C++ and, 42
defined, 42
illustrated, 43
in OOPLs, 42
See also Binding; Overloading; Virtual functions

Programming languages
enabling, 12
object-based, 15
supportive, 12
See also OOPL; *specific languages*

R

RPG/400
data structures, 15
file manipulation, 15
file type, 10
encapsulation and, 26
name overloading in, 40

S

SAVF class, 34
inheritance, 35

Simula, 49
objects in, 49

Smalltalk, 3, 35, 50
usage of, 51

SPACE class, 34

Static binding, 41

Subclass, 33

Superclass, 33
redefining, method, 36

U

User-defined data type, 10
Ada and, 10
module concept vs., 12

V

Virtual function, 72-74
defining, 73
program output, 74
runtime type and, 72
See also Polymorphism

Also Published by *NEWS/400*

Visit our web site at **www.dukepress.com**
for a more detailed listing of all Duke Press books

THE A TO Z OF EDI

By Nahid M. Jilovec

Electronic Data Interchange (EDI) can help reduce administrative costs, accelerate information processing, ensure data accuracy, and streamline business procedures. Here's a comprehensive guide to EDI to help in planning, startup, and implementation. The author reveals all the benefits, challenges, standards, and implementation secrets gained through extensive experience. She shows how to evaluate your business procedures, select special hardware and software, establish communications requirements and standards, address audit issues, and employ the legal support necessary for EDI activities. 263 pages.

APPLICATION DEVELOPER'S HANDBOOK FOR THE AS/400

Edited by Mike Otey, a **NEWS/400** *technical editor*

Explains how to effectively use the AS/400 to build reliable, flexible, and efficient business applications. Contains RPG/400 and CL coding examples and tips, and provides both step-by-step instructions and handy reference material. Includes diskette. 768 pages, 48 chapters.

AS/400 DISK SAVING TIPS & TECHNIQUES

By James R. Plunkett

Want specific help for cleaning up and maintaining your disk? Here are more than 50 tips, plus design techniques for minimizing your disk usage. Each tip is completely explained with the "symptom," the problem, and the technique or code you need to correct it. 72 pages.

AS/400 SUBFILES IN RPG

On the AS/400, subfiles are powerful and easy to use, and with this book you can start working with subfiles in just a few hours — no need to wade through page after page of technical jargon. You'll start with the concept behind subfiles, then discover how easy they are to program. The book contains all of the DDS subfile keywords announced in V2R3 of OS/400. Five complete RPG subfile programs are included, and the book comes complete with a 3.5" PC diskette containing all those programs plus DDS. The book is an updated version of the popular *Programming Subfiles in RPG/400.* 200 pages, 4 chapters.

C FOR RPG PROGRAMMERS

By Jennifer Hamilton, a **NEWS/400** *author*

Written from the perspective of an RPG programmer, this book includes side-by-side coding examples written in both C and RPG to aid comprehension and understanding, clear identification of unique C constructs, and a comparison of RPG op-codes to equivalent C concepts. Includes many tips and examples covering the use of C/400. 292 pages, 23 chapters.

CL BY EXAMPLE

By Virgil Green

CL by Example gives programmers and operators more than 850 pages of practical information you can use in your day-to-day job. It's full of application examples, tips, and techniques, along with a sprinkling of humor. The examples will speed you through the learning curve to help you become a more proficient, more productive CL programmer. 864 pages, 12 chapters.

CLIENT ACCESS TOKEN-RING CONNECTIVITY

By Chris Patterson

Attaching PCs to AS/400s via a Token-Ring can become a complicated subject — when things go wrong, an understanding of PCs, the Token-Ring, and OS/400 is often required. *Client Access Token-Ring Connectivity* details all that is required in these areas to successfully maintain and trouble-shoot a Token-Ring network. The first half of the book introduces the Token-Ring and describes the Client Access communications architecture, the Token-Ring connection from both the PC side and the AS/400 side, and the Client Access applications. The second half provides a useful guide to Token-Ring management, strategies for Token-Ring error identification and recovery, and tactics for resolving Client Access error messages. 125 pages, 10 chapters.

COMMON-SENSE C

Advice and warnings for C and C++ programmers

By Paul Conte, a **NEWS/400** *technical editor*

C programming language has its risks; this book shows how C programmers get themselves into trouble, includes tips to help you avoid C's pitfalls, and suggests how to manage C and C++ application development. 100 pages, 9 chapters.

CONTROL LANGUAGE PROGRAMMING FOR THE AS/400

By Bryan Meyers and Dan Riehl, **NEWS/400** *technical editors*

This comprehensive CL programming textbook offers students up-to-the-minute knowledge of the skills they will need in today's MIS environment. Progresses methodically from CL basics to more complex processes and concepts, guiding readers toward a professional grasp of CL programming techniques and style. 512 pages, 25 chapters.

DDS BY EXAMPLE

By R S Tipton

DDS by Example provides detailed coverage on the creation of physical files, field reference files, logical files, display files, and printer files. It includes more than 300 real-life examples, including examples of physical files, simple logical files, multi-format logical files, dynamic selection options, coding subfiles, handling overrides, creating online help, creating reports, and coding windows. 360 pages, 4 chapters.

DDS PROGRAMMING FOR DISPLAY & PRINTER FILES

By James Coolbaugh

Offers a thorough, straightforward explanation of how to use Data Description Specifications (DDS) to program display files and printer files. Covers basic to complex tasks using DDS functions. The author uses DDS programming examples for CL and RPG extensively throughout the book, and you can put these examples to use immediately. Focuses on topics such as general screen presentations, the A specification, defining data on the screen, record-format and field definitions, defining data fields, using indicators, data and text attributes, cursor and keyboard control, editing data, validity checking, response keywords, and function keys. A complimentary diskette includes all the source code presented in the book. 446 pages, 13 chapters.

DESKTOP GUIDE TO THE S/36

By Mel Beckman, Gary Kratzer, and Roger Pence, **NEWS/400** *technical editors*

This definitive S/36 survival manual includes practical techniques to supercharge your S/36, including ready-to-use information for maximum system performance tuning, effective application development, and smart Disk Data Management. Includes a review of two popular Unix-based S/36 work-alike migration alternatives. Diskette contains ready-to-run utilities to help you save machine time and implement power programming techniques such as External Program Calls. 387 pages, 21 chapters.

THE ESSENTIAL GUIDE TO CLIENT ACCESS FOR DOS EXTENDED

By John Enck, Robert E. Anderson, and Michael Otey

The Essential Guide to Client Access for DOS Extended contains key insights and need-to-know technical information about Client Access for DOS Extended, IBM's strategic AS/400 product for DOS and Windows client/server connectivity. This book provides background information about the history and architecture of Client Access for DOS Extended; fundamental information about how to install and configure Client Access; and advanced information about integrating Client Access with other types of networks, managing how Client Access for DOS Extended operates under Windows, and developing client/server applications with Client Access. Written by industry experts based on their personal and professional experiences with Client Access, this book can help you avoid time-consuming pitfalls that litter the path of AS/400 client/server computing. 430 pages, 12 chapters.

ILE: A FIRST LOOK

By George Farr and Shailan Topiwala

This book begins by showing the differences between ILE and its predecessors, then goes on to explain the essentials of an ILE program — using concepts such as modules, binding, service programs, and binding directories. You'll discover how ILE program activation works and how ILE works with its predecessor environments. The book covers the new APIs and new debugging facilities and explains the benefits of ILE's new exception-handling model. You also get answers to the most commonly asked questions about ILE. 183 pages, 9 chapters.

IMPLEMENTING AS/400 SECURITY, SECOND EDITION

A practical guide to implementing, evaluating, and auditing your AS/400 security strategy

By Wayne Madden, a **NEWS/400** *technical editor*

Concise and practical, this second edition brings together in one place the fundamental AS/400 security tools and experience-based recommendations that you need and also includes specifics on the latest security enhancements available in OS/400 Version 3 Release 1. Completely updated from the first edition, this is the only source for the latest information about how to protect your system against attack from its increasing exposure to hackers. 389 pages, 16 chapters.

INSIDE THE AS/400

An in-depth look at the AS/400's design, architecture, and history

By Frank G. Soltis

The inside story every AS/400 developer has been waiting for, told by Dr. Frank G. Soltis, IBM's AS/400 chief architect. Never before has IBM provided an in-depth look at the AS/400's design, architecture, and history. This authoritative book does just that — and also looks at some of the people behind the scenes who created this revolutionary system for you. Whether you are an executive looking for a high-level overview or a "bit-twiddling techie" who wants all the details, *Inside the AS/400* demystifies this system, shedding light on how it came to be, how it can do the things it does, and what its future may hold — especially in light of its new PowerPC RISC processors. 475 pages, 12 chapters.

AN INTRODUCTION TO COMMUNICATIONS FOR THE AS/400, SECOND EDITION

By John Enck and Ruggero Adinolfi

This second edition has been revised to address the sweeping communications changes introduced with V3R1 of OS/400. As a result, this book now covers the broad range of AS/400 communications technology topics, ranging from Ethernet to X.25, and from APPN to AnyNet. The book presents an introduction to data communications and then covers communications fundamentals, types of networks, OSI, SNA, APPN, networking roles, the AS/400 as host and server, TCP/IP, and the AS/400-DEC connection. 210 pages, 13 chapters.

JIM SLOAN'S CL TIPS & TECHNIQUES

By Jim Sloan, developer of QUSRTOOL's TAA Tools

Written for those who understand CL, this book draws from Jim Sloan's knowledge and experience as a developer for the S/38 and the AS/400, and his creation of QUSRTOOL's TAA tools, to give you tips that can help you write better CL programs and become more productive. Includes more than 200 field-tested techniques, plus exercises to help you understand and apply many of the techniques presented. 564 pages, 30 chapters.

MASTERING THE AS/400

A practical, hands-on guide

By Jerry Fottral

This introductory textbook to AS/400 concepts and facilities has a utilitarian approach that stresses student participation. A natural prerequisite to programming and database management courses, it emphasizes mastery of system/user interface, member-object-library relationship, utilization of CL commands, and basic database and program development utilities. Also includes labs focusing on essential topics such as printer spooling; library lists; creating and maintaining physical files; using logical files; using CL and DDS; working in the PDM environment; and using SEU, DFU, Query, and SDA. 484 pages, 12 chapters.

OBJECT-ORIENTED PROGRAMMING FOR AS/400 PROGRAMMERS

By Jennifer Hamilton, a **NEWS/400** *author*

Explains basic OOP concepts such as classes and inheritance in simple, easy-to-understand terminology. The OS/400 object-oriented architecture serves as the basis for the discussion throughout, and concepts presented are reinforced through an introduction to the C++ object-oriented programming language, using examples based on the OS/400 object model. 114 pages, 14 chapters.

PERFORMANCE PROGRAMMING — MAKING RPG SIZZLE

By Mike Dawson, CDP

Mike Dawson spent more than two years preparing this book — evaluating programming options, comparing techniques, and establishing benchmarks on thousands of programs. "Using the techniques in this book," he says, "I have made program after program run 30%, 40%, even 50% faster." To help you do the same, Mike gives you code and benchmark results for initializing and clearing arrays, performing string manipulation, using validation arrays with look-up techniques, using arrays in arithmetic routines, and a lot more. 257 pages, 8 chapters.

POWER TOOLS FOR THE AS/400, VOLUMES I AND II

Edited by Frederick L. Dick and Dan Riehl

NEWS 3X/400's Power Tools for the AS/400 is a two-volume reference series for people who work with the AS/400. Volume I (originally titled *AS/400 Power Tools*) is a collection of the best tools, tips, and techniques published in *NEWS/34-38* (pre-August 1988) and *NEWS 3X/400* (August 1988 through October 1991) that are applicable to the AS/400. *Volume II* extends this original collection by including material that appeared through 1994. Each book includes a diskette that provides load-and-go code for easy-to-use solutions to many everyday problems. *Volume I*: 709 pages, 24 chapters; *Volume II*: 702 pages, 14 chapters.

PROGRAMMING IN RPG IV

By Judy Yaeger, Ph.D., a **NEWS/400** *technical editor*

This textbook provides a strong foundation in the essentials of business programming, featuring the newest version of the RPG language: RPG IV. Focuses on real-world problems and down-to-earth solutions using the latest techniques and features of RPG. Provides everything you need to know to write a well-designed RPG IV program. Each chapter includes informative, easy-to-read explanations and examples as well as a section of thought-provoking questions, exercises, and programming assignments. Four appendices and a handy, comprehensive glossary support the topics presented throughout the book. An instructor's kit is available. 450 pages, 13 chapters.

PROGRAMMING IN RPG/400, SECOND EDITION

By Judy Yaeger, Ph.D., a **NEWS/400** *technical editor*

This second edition refines and extends the comprehensive instructional material contained in the original textbook and features a new section that introduces externally described printer files, a new chapter that highlights the fundamentals of RPG IV, and a new appendix that correlates the key concepts from each chapter with their RPG IV counterparts. Includes everything you need to learn how to write a well-designed RPG program, from the most basic to the more complex, and each chapter includes a section of questions, exercises, and programming assignments that reinforce the knowledge you have gained from the chapter and strengthen the groundwork for succeeding chapters. An instructor's kit is available. 440 pages, 14 chapters.

PROGRAMMING SUBFILES IN COBOL/400

By Jerry Goldson

Learn how to program subfiles in COBOL/400 in a matter of hours! This powerful and flexible programming technique no longer needs to elude you. You can begin programming with subfiles the same day you get the book. You don't have to wade through page after page, chapter after chapter of rules and parameters and keywords. Instead, you get solid, helpful information and working examples that you can apply to your application programs right away. 204 pages, 5 chapters.

THE QUINTESSENTIAL GUIDE TO PC SUPPORT

By John Enck, Robert E. Anderson, Michael Otey, and Michael Ryan

This comprehensive book about IBM's AS/400 PC Support connectivity product defines the architecture of PC Support and its role in midrange networks, describes PC Support's installation and configuration procedures, and shows you how you can configure and use PC Support to solve real-life problems. 345 pages, 11 chapters.

RPG ERROR HANDLING TECHNIQUE

Bulletproofing Your Applications

By Russell Popeil

RPG Error Handling Technique teaches you the skills you need to use the powerful tools provided by OS/400 and RPG to handle almost any error from within your programs. The book explains the INFSR, INFDS, PSSR, and SDS in programming terms, with examples that show you how all these tools work together and which tools are most appropriate for which kind of error or exception situation. It continues by presenting a robust suite of error/exception handling techniques within RPG programs. Each technique is explained in an application setting, using both RPG III and RPG IV code. 164 pages, 5 chapters.

RPG IV BY EXAMPLE

By George Farr and Shailan Topiwala

RPG IV by Example addresses the needs and concerns of RPG programmers at any level of experience. The focus is on RPG IV in a practical context that lets AS/400 professionals quickly grasp what's new without dwelling on the old. Beginning with an overview of RPG IV specifications, the authors prepare the way for examining all the features of the new version of the language. The chapters that follow explore RPG IV further with practical, easy-to-use applications. 500 pages, 15 chapters.

RPG IV JUMP START

Moving ahead with the new RPG

By Bryan Meyers, a **NEWS/400** *technical editor*

Introducing the "new" RPG, in which the columnar syntax has been challenged (all the specifications have changed, some vestigial specifications from an earlier era have been eliminated, and new specifications and data types have been added), this book shows you RPG IV from the perspective of a programmer who already knows the old RPG. Points out the differences between the two and demonstrates how to take advantage of the new syntax and function. 193 pages, 12 chapters.

RPG/400 INTERACTIVE TEMPLATE TECHNIQUE

By Carson Soule, CDP, CCP, CSP

Here's an updated version of Carson Soule's *Interactive RPG/400 Programming*. The book shows you time-saving, program-sharpening concepts behind the template approach, and includes all the code you need to build one perfect program after another. These templates include code for cursor-sensitive prompting in DDS, for handling messages in resident RPG programs, for using the CLEAR opcode to eliminate hard-coded field initialization, and much more. There's even a new select template with a pop-up window. 258 pages, 10 chapters.

S/36 POWER TOOLS

Edited by Chuck Lundgren, a **NEWS/400** *technical editor*

Winner of an STC Award of Achievement in 1992, this book contains five years' worth of articles, tips, and programs published in *NEWS 3X/400* from 1986 to October 1990, including more than 290 programs and procedures. Extensively cross-referenced for fast and easy problem solving, and complete with diskette containing all the programming code. 737 pages, 20 chapters.

STARTER KIT FOR THE AS/400, SECOND EDITION

An indispensable guide for novice to intermediate AS/400 programmers and system operators

By Wayne Madden, a **NEWS/400** *technical editor*

with contributions by Bryan Meyers, Andrew Smith, and Peter Rowley

This second edition contains updates of the material in the first edition and incorporates new material to enhance it's value as a resource to help you learn important basic concepts and nuances of the AS/400 system. New material focuses on installing a new release, working with PTFs, AS/400 message handling, working with and securing printed output, using operational assistant to manage disk space, job scheduling, save and restore basics, and more basic CL programming concepts. Optional diskette available. 429 pages, 33 chapters.

SUBFILE TECHNIQUE FOR RPG/400 PROGRAMMERS

By Jonathan Yergin, CDP, and Wayne Madden

Here's the code you need for a complete library of shell subfile programs: RPG/400 code, DDS, CL, and sample data files. There's even an example for programming windows. You even get some "whiz bang" techniques that add punch to your applications. This book explains the code in simple, straightforward style and tells you when each technique should be used for best results. 326 pages, 11 chapters, 3.5" PC diskette included.

TECHNICAL REFERENCE SERIES

Edited by Bryan Meyers, a **NEWS/400** *technical editor*

Written by experts — such as John Enck, Bryan Meyers, Julian Monypenny, Roger Pence, Dan Riehl — these unique desktop guides put the latest AS/400 applications and techniques at your fingertips. These "just-do-it" books (featuring wire-o binding to open flat at every page) are priced so you can keep your personal set handy. Optional online Windows help diskette available for each book.

Desktop Guide to CL Programming

By Bryan Meyers, a **NEWS/400** *technical editor*

This first book of the **NEWS/400** *Technical Reference Series* is packed with easy-to-find notes, short explanations, practical tips, answers to most of your everyday questions about CL, and CL code segments you can use in your own CL programming. Complete "short reference" lists every command and explains the most-often-used ones, along with names of the files they use and the MONMSG messages to use with them. 205 pages, 36 chapters.

Desktop Guide to AS/400 Programmers' Tools

By Dan Riehl, a **NEWS/400** *technical editor*

This second book of the **NEWS/400** *Technical Reference Series* gives you the "how-to" behind all the tools included in *Application Development ToolSet/400* (ADTS/400), IBM's Licensed Program Product for Version 3 of OS/400; includes Source Entry Utility (SEU), Programming Development Manager (PDM), Screen Design Aid (SDA), Report Layout Utility (RLU), File Compare/Merge Utility (FCMU) — *new in V3R1*, and Interactive Source Debugger — *new in V3R1*. Highlights topics and functions specific to Version 3 of OS/400. 266 pages, 30 chapters.

Desktop Guide to DDS

By James Coolbaugh

This third book of the **NEWS/400** *Technical Reference Series* provides a complete reference to all DDS keywords for physical, logical, display, printer, and ICF files. Each keyword is briefly explained, with syntax rules and examples showing how to code the keyword. All basic and pertinent information is provided for quick and easy access. While this guide explains every parameter for a keyword, it doesn't explain every possible exception that might exist. Rather, the guide includes the basics about what each keyword is designed to accomplish. The *Desktop Guide to DDS* is designed to give quick, "at your fingertips" information about every keyword — with this in hand, you won't need to refer to IBM's bulky *DDS Reference* manual. 132 pages, 5 major sections.

Desktop Guide to RPG/400

By Roger Pence and Julian Monypenny, **NEWS/400** *technical editors*

This fourth book in the *Technical Reference Series* provides a variety of RPG templates, subroutines, and copy modules, sprinkled with evangelical advice, that will help you write robust and effective RPG/400 programs. Highlights of the information provided include string-handling routines, numeric editing routines, date routines, error-handling modules, tips for using OS/400 APIs with RPG/400, and interactive programming techniques. For all types of RPG projects, this book's tested and ready-to-run building blocks will easily snap into your RPG. The programming solutions provided here would otherwise take you days or even weeks to write and test.

Desktop Guide to Creating CL Commands

By Lynn Nelson

In this most recent book in the *Technical Reference Series*, author Lynn Nelson shows you how to create your own CL commands with the same functionality and power as the IBM commands you use every day, including automatic parameter editing, all the function keys, F4 prompt for values, expanding lists of values, and conditional prompting. After you have read this book, you can write macros for the operations you do over and over every day or write application commands that prompt users for essential information. Whether you're in operations or programming, don't miss this opportunity to enhance your career-building skills. 164 pages, 14 chapters.

UNDERSTANDING BAR CODES

By James R. Plunkett

One of the most important waves of technology sweeping American industry is the use of bar coding to capture and track data. The wave is powered by two needs: the need to gather information in a more accurate and timely manner and the need to track that information once it is gathered. Bar coding meets these needs and provides creative and cost-effective solutions for many applications. With so many leading-edge technologies, it can be difficult for IS professionals to keep up with the concepts and applications they need to make solid decisions. This book gives you an overview of bar code technology including a discussion of the bar codes themselves, the hardware that supports bar coding, how and when to justify and then implement a bar code application, plus examples of many different applications and how bar coding can be used to solve problems. 70 pages.

USING QUERY/400

By Patrice Gapen and Catherine Stoughton

This textbook, designed for any AS/400 user from student to professional with or without prior programming knowledge, presents Query as an easy and fast tool for creating reports and files from AS/400 databases. Topics are ordered from simple to complex and emphasize hands-on AS/400 use; they include defining database files to Query, selecting and sequencing fields, generating new numeric and character fields, sorting within Query, joining database files, defining custom headings, creating new database files, and more. Instructor's kit available. 92 pages, 10 chapters.

USING VISUAL BASIC WITH CLIENT ACCESS APIs

By Ron Jones

This book is for programmers who want to develop client/server solutions on the AS/400 and the personal computer. Whether you are a VB novice or a VB expert, you will gain by reading this book because it provides a thorough overview of the pinciples and requirements for programming in Windows using VB. Companion diskettes contain source code for all the programming projects referenced in the book, as well as for numerous other utilities and programs. All the projects are compatible with Windows 95 and VB 4.0. 680 pages, 13 chapters.

FOR A COMPLETE CATALOG OR TO PLACE AN ORDER, CONTACT

NEWS/400
Duke Communications International
221 E. 29th Street • Loveland, CO 80538-2727
(800) 621-1544 • (970) 663-4700 • Fax: (970) 669-3016